9

THE DAYSTAR VOYAGES

THE WHITE DRAGON OF SHARNU

GILBERT MORRIS
AND DAN MEEKS

MOODY PRESS
CHICAGO

© 2000 by
GILBERT MORRIS
AND
DANIEL MEEKS

ISBN: 0-8024-4109-2

1 3 5 7 9 10 8 6 4 2

Printed in the United States of America

I dedicate this book to my beautiful daughter Gina Marie Kruger and her handsome husband, Boyd.

A parent dreams that his children will find love and happiness in life and that the persons they marry will be handpicked by God.

We are most fortunate, because our daughter Gina married such a man. We love you guys!

—*Dad (and Mom)*
[Dan Meeks]

Characters

The *Daystar* .... an intergalactic star cruiser

The *Daystar* Space Rangers:
Jerusha Ericson, 15 .... a topflight engineer
Raina St. Clair, 14 .... the ship's communications officer
Mei-Lani Lao, 13 .... *Daystar*'s historian and linguist
Ringo Smith, 14 .... a computer wizard
Heck Jordan, 15 .... an electronics genius
Dai Bando, 16 .... known for his exceptional physical abilities

The *Daystar* Officers:
Mark Edge .... *Daystar*'s young captain
Zeno Thrax .... the first officer
Bronwen Llewellen .... the navigator; Dai's aunt
Ivan Petroski .... the chief engineer
Temple Cole .... the flight surgeon
Tara Jaleel .... the weapons officer
Studs Cagney .... the crew chief

Contents

1

On Board the *Daystar*

Mei-Lani Lao stood on the *Daystar*'s bridge with her close friend Raina St. Clair. Under her feet the intergalactic cruiser wheeled through space, speeding toward Polaris, Earth's designated "North Star." The bridge was quiet as the girls performed routine system's checks. It was imperative that they keep the ship in top condition, for they never knew what dangers awaited them in deep space.

As Raina's nimble fingers raced over the navigation controls, Mei-Lani suddenly stopped working. Thoughtfully, she rested her right hand on her chin and looked through the portal.

Mei-Lani was the youngest of the *Daystar* Space Rangers. She was Asian. Her hair was black, and her eyes were warm and brown. She was a small girl, barely more than five feet and weighing only ninety-five pounds. But what Mei-Lani lacked in size she made up in brains. She was a historian and a language expert. She could learn two languages more easily than most people could learn one.

After a moment she turned thoughtfully to her companion and said, "Raina, I've been thinking a lot about our last mission. And I confess I'm still a little confused."

Raina St. Clair stopped her work on the console to look at her. Raina was a frail appearing girl with an oval face highlighted by a cleft in her chin. Mei-Lani had long been convinced that Raina was the most devout Space Ranger on the cruiser. She seemed to know much of the Bible by heart.

"What bothers you about our last mission?" Raina asked.

Mei-Lani told her. She had been thinking of the strange sickness that had come out of nowhere and had almost taken her life. "The whole thing just seemed too mysterious, that's all. I still don't understand it."

Raina shrugged and went back to work. "Well, galactic medical technology is still lacking in many areas. A lot of people mistakenly think that medical science always has all the answers to everything, but there are just a lot of mysteries out there. Even in the space age. Only God has all the answers, but we can be sure He does."

"I'm just grateful that the ancient Amesstorites knew how to treat whatever it was I had," Mei-Lani said. She turned back to the portal, remembering Primal One—the robot leader of the planet Throsis, who transferred the Amesstorite medical database into the *Daystar*'s computer. Fortunately, that long-extinct race had discovered the way to neutralize the effects of Denebian radiation. It was that information that had saved Mei-Lani's life.

She thought of the Denebians. They were a hostile race. In fact, they attacked anyone and everyone who ventured into their space. Many believed that the Denebians were even responsible for the annihilation of the Amesstorites thousands of years ago. Galactic Command steered clear of the Denebians, for a battle with them would be very costly indeed.

Now Mei-Lani smoothed her black hair with a hand. "It seems to me there are about as many things that are still mysteries to galactic scientists as what they know. But maybe some things are meant to be unknown. Maybe people just aren't *supposed* to have an answer for everything." She nodded vigorously and went on. "For example, Dr. Cole—with all her medical knowledge and all her computers—couldn't even diagnose my problem, much less cure me. But I put my life in God's hands, no matter what the consequences. And you saw what He did."

"And you did the right thing," Raina agreed quickly with a smile. She reached over and lay a hand on Mei-Lani's shoulder. "Trusting God all the time—and not just when a person's facing a life-or-death situation—that's exactly what He wants us to do. And He sure uses strange things to help us at times—things that we'd never think of. Who would have ever guessed that the Amesstorite medical banks would have had the answers Dr. Cole needed?"

The two girls worked quietly for a while longer, and then Raina gave Mei-Lani a fond look. "I felt so hopeless when I thought you were going to die. It was hard for me to leave the problem with God to do what was best. I don't think I've ever been so short on faith."

Mei-Lani grinned broadly. Raina was older than she was, but Mei-Lani had always felt very close to her anyway. "Well, here I am," she said. "Take a good look at me. I'm not dead. I'm not even sick anymore. And God did it."

Raina nodded slowly. "He certainly did. But back to the mysterious part—I still think part of the problem was that Shiva statue."

Shiva. The goddess that was worshiped by Tara Jaleel, the *Daystar*'s weapons officer. Raina had always said that anything to do with Shiva was deadly.

"You really think that dust from the Shiva statue brought that sickness on me?"

Raina shrugged. "I think of *any* idols as time bombs. If you keep one of them around, sooner or later something is going to go bad. There's evil in all of them, Mei-Lani."

"Well, I've wondered a lot about those Denebian people. We don't know much about them. We don't even know why they glow with that green light. But we do know now that the Shiva statue was made in Deneb."

Raina grunted in agreement. "And who knows how many kinds of radiation and mutated elements exist in Deneb—not found anywhere else in the galaxy." She made a minor adjustment on the communications console, then went on. "I talked to Bronwen one day about it all."

"What did she say?"

"She said she thinks God lets some things happen in life just to shake us up—to give our faith in Him a chance to grow. He is the only one who knows what the next day will bring to anybody. And He has nothing in mind for us but good. We never make a mistake by trusting Him."

"Bronwen's right. She always is." Mei-Lani smiled at the thought of *Daystar*'s navigator. Most of the young Space Rangers looked on this older woman almost as a mother.

"When my parents died, though," Mei-Lani said thoughtfully, "I had a hard time believing that God is good."

"I never knew that."

"Well, I did. But I kept praying to Him no matter how bad I felt, and He brought me through that time. He still helps me today when I get sad about my parents. Without the Lord I wouldn't have made it this far."

Raina squeezed Mei-Lani's shoulder. "Neither would I."

Heck Jordan was helping the chief engineer with the safety links located in the bowels of Engineering.

These links were the fuses that protected the relay paths from the engineering computers to the main Star Drive engines.

"Open the access panel, Heck," Ivan Petroski ordered gruffly.

Heck opened the latches, and the large red panel promptly fell to the deck, almost hitting Ivan on the head.

"Be careful!" the chief engineer yelped in surprise.

"I'm sorry. I didn't mean for that to happen. The stupid panel fell before I could grab it." Heck was obviously getting tired of taking Ivan's grouchy orders.

Ivan Petroski knew he was often cranky. Sometimes his anger was bigger than he was. The engineer was no more than four feet six, though he was well proportioned. He had flashing brown eyes and thick brown hair. He came from Belinka Two, where everyone was about his size. Indeed, he often boasted that he was one of the tallest men there. As chief engineer, he had great responsibility on the *Daystar*, and one of his biggest problems always turned out to be Heck Jordan.

"I'd like to open the hatch and throw you out into space!" Ivan grumbled crossly. He had no respect for this reckless young man who gave him so much trouble. Ivan felt like a baby-sitter.

Heck Jordan was a heavyset boy with bright red hair and innocent-looking blue eyes. He was an electronics genius, but he had several serious problems. He ate constantly—usually sweets—and Ivan Petroski was sure he was the most selfish human being on board the ship. Ivan well knew that Heck was very stubborn and was mostly concerned about getting his own way. When you added to all his bad habits the fact that he loved fancy clothes but was color-blind, Heck was a very noticeable young man.

Right now he was tugging at the lime green neckerchief that ill-suited his uniform—although of course he would not know that—and he paid no attention to the chief engineer.

Petroski yelled until he was almost hoarse. Finally, he decided that the ensign was going to totally ignore him. Ivan reached up and pulled free a very warm safety link from the relay tracks above his head. He tossed the link toward Heck.

Each safety link measured about two feet long and three inches in diameter. Twenty of these links were connected to circuit pathways behind the panel that Heck had just removed. Ivan figured that it was better to lose a safety link than to blow the engine computers. The condition of the safety links was OK, but the temperature of the operating links would make someone think twice about holding on to one for long.

Heck caught the hot link by reflex and then started juggling it wildly. "Hey, look out!" he yelled at Ivan. "What did you do that for? That's hot!"

Ivan grinned at the Ranger as Heck finally put the relay down and blew on his hands. "I wanted to make a point," Ivan told him.

"Well, you didn't have to burn my hands off!"

"Heck, you're irresponsible, and you won't follow orders."

Heck glared at the engineer. Then he picked up the cooling-down link and tossed it back to Ivan, who replaced it in its receptacle. Heck looked down at his red hands and blew on them again. "That hurt!"

"If you'd just do what you're supposed to be doing and stop acting like an idiot, I wouldn't try to burn you up."

Heck reached into a pocket and lazily brought out a candy bar. Then he unwrapped it and chewed off half in one bite. "Well, maybe I do have a problem, Ivan. Maybe."

"*A* problem! You got a hundred problems!" the chief engineer roared.

"It's just that I'm impulsive, and I want to get on with the program. Sometimes I don't always think things out before I act."

"Look, Heck," Ivan said a little more calmly, "I want to help you, but you've got to start listening. Nothing's going to get better on this ship until you start to pay attention."

"All right, then, Ivan. Go ahead and talk. I'm listening," Heck said. He turned back to his computer.

And Petroski knew that Ensign Heck Jordan immediately closed his ears to anything he was about say.

In the main computer room, Ringo Smith and Jerusha Ericson were combining their skills to shorten the input pathways to the main computer. Since these were the very brains of the star cruiser, only the most talented engineers and computer geniuses could touch a single circuit. The walls of the room were alive with activity as the banks of multicolored LEDs flashed on and off.

"Jerusha, I think if we can just get this input configuration going, it will make the *Daystar*'s computers really fly," Ringo said.

"You can do it if anybody can, Ringo," Jerusha said confidently. "You're the best with computers that I ever saw."

Jerusha was fifteen. Her ash-blonde hair hung down to her shoulders, and her blue eyes were so dark that sometimes they looked black. She had a squarish face and was tall and athletic. Some thought she was somewhat too competitive, but not Ringo Smith. He admired her greatly. He admired most pretty girls greatly.

Ringo considered himself to be average looking with average brown hair. As he talked to Jerusha, he fingered the medallion suspended around his neck on a leather thong. It bore the image of a bird of prey on one side, but on the other side was the image of his father—about whom he did not like to speak.

"I've been doing a lot of thinking about those robots back on Throsis, Jerusha. Especially Primal One." Even now he could picture in his mind those advanced robots. They had been almost humanlike in appearance.

Ringo could not get over his fascination with Primal One. In every way the head robot had acted very human, although he knew the machine was completely composed of advanced technology that had been given humanoid shape. Primal One had explained that their creators, the Amesstorites, believed that life could be created only by God. And Primal One was quick to state that the robot colony on Throsis was exactly that —a colony of robots.

"I've been thinking, Jerusha. Maybe somehow those *were* real people and not robots at all. They were just like real people. When you touched them, it was like touching real flesh, wasn't it?"

"No, they weren't real people. And no, Ringo, there was nothing about their metal skin that felt human. Go feel the computer housing over there." She pointed at a metal cabinet. "Does that feel like real flesh to you? No. The robots were highly advanced, but they were definitely not living."

"How do you know for sure? The Amesstorites have been dead for thousands of years. Maybe the robots started off as robots but then evolved into something more than just a piece of machinery."

Jerusha smiled at him, but she shook her head firmly. "Nope. No evolving. That can't be, Ringo. God is the one who created life. And for all their talk, the scientists have never produced one self-aware life-form."

"You're sure about that?"

"Of course I am. The Bible says that God created man 'in His own image.' No one can manufacture the image of God."

Ringo shifted slightly, made an adjustment on his computer, and decided to change the subject. "Have you noticed anything funny about Raina lately?"

"What do you mean, 'funny'? You mean funny peculiar?"

"Yeah. I think there's something bothering her, but I don't know what it is. Have you noticed?"

Jerusha brushed back her hair and hesitated before she answered. Then she said, "Well, it's been a long time since Raina and I have had a good talk. Maybe I ought to spend more time with her. Find out how she's doing."

Ringo suddenly asked, "Jerusha, did you ever like someone who didn't like you?"

Jerusha laughed aloud. She had a very attractive laugh, and her teeth shone white against her tanned skin. "Ringo, that's been the story of my romantic life."

"What do you mean?" Ringo was dying to hear a Jerusha love story.

"Never mind what I mean," she replied promptly. "When you're a lot older, I might tell you a story or two." But she smiled again. "For now, all I'm going to admit is that I haven't been too lucky with love."

2

A White Dragon

The astrophysics lab was the dullest looking room aboard the spaceship. The floor, walls, and ceiling were all painted a flat blue, and the room looked more like a jail cell than one of the most advanced technical centers on *Daystar*.

"I just can't get used to a room that has no corners," Dai Bando complained as he, Mei-Lani, and Bronwen Llewellen entered.

"I agree with you, nephew," Bronwen said. "But of course this room wouldn't work right if there were corners."

Mei-Lani smiled at him. "Dai, this machine generates star fields. It has to reflect the appearance of infinity. To have corners to the room would hinder the effect."

"Enough already, you two," Dai said good-naturedly. "I'm the first to admit that even a cargo rat has more brains than I do. But, please—give me a break. I *know* the reason there aren't corners in here. All I said was that it feels odd."

His aunt gave Dai a big hug as Mei-Lani pressed the control switch that raised the control panel from its location in the center of the floor.

"What coordinates do you want me to input?" she asked Bronwen.

"Bring up Polaris."

"You could see Polaris on the bridge viewer if you wanted to, Bronwen," Mei-Lani volunteered. "We're headed straight for it."

17

The navigator gave the girl an affectionate smile. "I know, but I want to study the star systems around Polaris."

Mei-Lani pressed the appropriate switches, and the dull blue room turned into one full of stars, separated by the darkness of space. Even the floor now had the appearance of stars.

The effect made Dai feel as if he were floating in space. His inner ear equilibrium was distorting the visual signals his eyes were sending to his brain. "Whoopee!" he yelled. "This is neat."

"Neat?" Mei-Lani repeated. She was obviously trying not to laugh. "I suspect no one has used the word 'neat' in a very long time."

Dai was only a little embarrassed. "At least one person uses it. *I* use it. So there. Neat is a neat word—don't you think?"

Bronwen threw up her hands and interrupted them. "If you two keep this up, we won't get any work done at all. Now, first, help me map out the navigational settings of the Draco constellation."

"Draco?" Mei-Lani asked curiously. "I thought we were headed toward Polaris."

"You're right about that," the navigator answered. "We are headed toward Polaris. But if I know our friend Commandant Lee, we'd better be prepared for the unexpected. I found myself in Draco a few years back, and I had a very strange experience as we flew through that sector."

"What kind of strange experience?" Dai asked curiously. He couldn't help noticing that his aunt's expression had turned unusually serious.

But Bronwen walked to the display of the Draco constellation and pointed at the string of stars that encircled Polaris. "This system is one of the most famous of any in Earth mythology." She studied the string of stars thoughtfully. "Each planet has a story of its own about dragons. And none of them is any stranger than Earth's legends about the Draco sector."

Mei-Lani, the historian, walked over to stand next to Bronwen. "Let me tell him, Bronwen. May I?"

"Go for it," Bronwen said as she smiled her approval.

Mei-Lani looked at Dai. Her eyes were wide with excitement as she began the story. "Many, many years ago—back in Earth's early history—there was a city that was called Babylon. Well, the ancient priests of Babylon made up wild stories about the heavens to explain things that were mysteries to mankind at that time. But everyone believed that the priests were telling the truth."

Dai grinned. "And the priests were really just liars, right?"

"I suppose they were, but a lot of our own beliefs about space today are still just theories. Does that make us liars, too?" Mei-Lani asked.

"I guess not, but the priests should have said that their stories were just guesses."

"And I agree with that," Bronwen put in. "The truth should be supported by facts, not educated guesses. When we *are* guessing, we should say so."

"Then the ruler of Babylon wanted to know how the earth and sky were made," Mei-Lani went on. "The priests were really in a dilemma. If they didn't give the ruler a good answer, they could wind up dead."

Dai saw his aunt smile knowingly at Mei-Lani. She obviously knew the story well, but this was the first Dai had heard it.

"So the priests told the ruler a story—a made-up story—that the ruler could neither prove nor disprove." Mei-Lani stepped toward one bright star in the display and pointed toward it. "You see this star?"

"Of course, Mei-Lani. All three of us can see it. And I might add," Dai said with a twinkle, "that it looks pretty neat."

"The star is named Thuban, and it used to be Earth's 'North Star' thousands and thousands of years ago. In those days the whole Draco constellation seemed to be slithering around Thuban like a serpent."

Bronwen switched some controls that made Thuban appear stationary, while Draco orbited around it.

"But that is much different from what we see from Earth today," Dai said.

"Exactly!" both females cried in unison.

"But I still don't understand one thing." Dai swiveled his head in a circle watching Draco's journey around Thuban. "What does all this have to do with the priests' answer?"

"The priests told the ruler that the goddess Taimet had created fearsome monsters to help her. And then, they said, eventually she turned herself into a dragon. According to the story, the whole earth was filled with lawlessness and chaos until a hero named Marduk came along. He defeated Taimet by commanding strong winds to blow into her dragon mouth. That split her body in two."

"And that killed her," Dai concluded.

"Not at all. One half of her became the sky, and the other half turned into Earth." Mei-Lani then pointed back at the Draco constellation. "And she's been there ever since, in the form of a constellation."

Dai whistled in astonishment. "You sure have a lot of knowledge locked into that pretty head of yours." He gave her a brotherly hug. "So did the ruler believe what the priests told him?"

"Of course he did." Bronwen answered this time. "And the same story was picked up by many peoples— the Greeks, the Indians, the Egyptians, to name a few. In fact the Egyptians faced one of their temples toward Thuban. There are several variations of the story in different places on Earth, of course, but it's still the same myth."

Dai found himself growing a little impatient with all this history. He was ready to get some work done, and he started pacing the deck. But then his mind turned to something else, and he looked at his aunt thoughtfully. "You said you'd once traveled through this part of space and had seen something strange in the Draco area."

"Yes, I certainly did," Bronwen said. She pointed to two stars that made up part of the dragon's head. "We were traveling between this double star— Rastaban—and its neighbor Eltanin, which, as you see, is the brightest star in the whole Draco constellation."

"Rastaban and Eltanin—names like those sound like some that were used in a book I read once," Mei-Lani interjected with a grin. *The Three Musketeers.*"

Bronwen laughed out loud. "I never thought of that, but I suppose you're right." She studied the twin stars. "Our mission was to introduce Galactic Command to the inhabitants of the planet SharNu, which orbits Eltanin." Looking at Mei-Lani, Bronwen continued by saying, "But it appears that your parents had already beaten us to SharNu."

"From their diaries, I know they went somewhere in the Draco sector."

"Do you know what they were searching for?" Bronwen asked.

"The notation I read said that they were trying to check out the story that dragons—white dragons—

roamed the space in the Draco sector for thousands of years."

"White dragons!" Dai exclaimed, stopping his pacing. "Why would they be white?"

"I don't know, Dai," Bronwen offered. "Why would they be any color? Who can say what a dragon looks like?"

"That's a good question," Mei-Lani said. "From my parents' diaries, I know they never saw one—white or otherwise. The only person I can think of that might have seen a dragon was a guy named Saint George."

Bronwen patted Mei-Lani's shoulder. "Again, that is a story that facts can't prove." Then she pointed to the space between Rastaban and Eltanin. "After a very good audience with King Regur and his beautiful wife, Queen Daleth, we departed from SharNu." She extended her index finger so that it touched the starlit wall. "We were still in SharNu's atmosphere when I saw something. I can't explain it. I just know that I was looking out the portal toward SharNu when, out of the corner of my eye, I thought I saw a large *lizard* fly past our ship. But when I turned my head to see, there was nothing there. I called the bridge and asked them to scan the area. They reported back that all scans were clear."

Dai's neck hairs seem to stand on end as his aunt continued.

"I turned back to the portal, and for just an instant there was this huge, white, reptilelike thing flying right toward me." Bronwen folded her arms on her chest and became silent.

"Then what?" Dai and Mei-Lani burst out.

"Whatever it was just . . . disappeared. But whatever it was that I saw could almost swallow *Daystar* whole!"

"Did the ship sound battle stations?" Dai's voice quivered with excitement. He loved action.

"There were no alarms, for no one saw the thing but me."

"You think it was a white dragon out in space? How could a dragon live in space? And can the white dragons make themselves invisible?" Mei-Lani asked.

"I just don't know. I don't have enough facts. But I know I saw *something*—for just a moment."

Dai turned to Mei-Lani. "Sounds pretty neat, doesn't it!"

Mei-Lani closed her hand into a fist and punched him on the arm.

Studs Cagney, his helper Myron, and a small crew of grunts were cleaning up *Daystar*'s training room. Studs was a bulky, broad man with a thickly muscled body. He was in charge of the grunts, the strong workers who took care of all nontechnical aspects of the spaceship.

While they worked, Studs kept a puzzled eye on Weapons Officer Tara Jaleel, who for some reason was prowling around the training room holding a small instrument in her hand. As she moved along, her fierce dark eyes never stopped. Her lips were drawn together in a straight line. She was an attractive woman in spite of her fierce features, but she had no friends on the spacecraft. Her worship of the goddess Shiva set her apart.

In appearance Jaleel was one of the most striking members of the *Daystar*'s crew. She was six feet tall and was a descendant of an old tribe of African warriors, the Masai. The Masai once had the reputation of being the fiercest warriors on Earth. No one could stand before them. Not many could stand before Tara Jaleel.

Studs glanced at Jaleel again and said in a whisper, "Myron, I have to say that's some woman officer. Did you ever see her in a fight?"

Myron nodded. "I have. She's too much, that one. Why, she could kill a man just with that martial arts chop of hers."

"Yeah." Studs grinned. "All the Space Rangers hate it when they have their Jai-Kando practice. Every one of them takes a beating."

"No, not all. Not Dai Bando," Myron said emphatically. "She's never laid a hand on him."

"Yeah, you're right," Studs said, rubbing his chin thoughtfully. "All but Bando. I've never seen anybody like that kid. He's quicker than a striking snake and stronger than I am—which is saying something."

"You and Bando had quite a run-in when he first came aboard, didn't you?"

"Yeah, I tried to put him down," Studs admitted, "but I couldn't do it. He could have flattened me anytime, but he didn't. I started kind of liking him after that."

Myron stopped his polishing of the equipment long enough to give Studs a sly grin. "He's gonna make a Christian out of you one of these days. You watch what I tell you."

Studs shot a hard glance at the grunt. But then he laughed. "Maybe so. I'd never even thought much about God until these Space Rangers came aboard. I expected I'd have to be running a nursery, but I've got to admit the kids are really something."

Myron and Studs discussed the Rangers for a minute or two, and then Myron abruptly asked, "Where do you reckon evil comes from, Studs?"

"Evil? I don't know. It's just here. Where did that question come from?"

"Well, it's those Denebians. They've got their share of it. I think they're the evilest people in the galaxy."

Studs finally shrugged. "It's my guess that the Denebians are probably descendants of a race called the Nishka. They're about as bad as you can get, all right. But the Denebians have been staying in their own sector, at least. Those Nishkas—they were an old spacefaring people that used to wipe out whole civilizations all over the galaxy." Studs eyebrows arched. "I ain't no historian, or nothing like that, but I've heard that—long ago—space was populated by races that had technology that was far more advanced than we've got today. It just got destroyed along the way somehow. Maybe them Denebians did it."

"What I can't figure out is what makes the Denebians so bad. There's no sense in it."

"They're a bad bunch all right," Studs agreed, and his eyes grew cloudy. An old memory came back to him, and his voice was tight as he said, "I was on a ship once that skirted the Denebian system. They about wiped us out."

"What did they do?"

"They bombarded us with trace elements of radioactive iridium three."

"What's that?"

"It's a rare isotope. They say it kills human beings quicker than you can smash a fly. But it breaks down quick, and after a short time you can't find any trace of it." He thought about that a moment, then said, "You know, maybe that's what happened to Mei-Lani."

"The little girl?"

"You know how sick she got. Nobody ever knew what it was. It could have been iridium three from Deneb, right in the lungs."

"Sounds bad. But it didn't kill her, so it couldn't have been that."

Studs scratched his head vigorously, still keeping his eye on Tara Jaleel at the same time. "I figure a whole Intergalactic Command ship could get bombarded with that stuff. It could kill everybody and then vanish. No one would ever know that the Denebians were involved."

Myron turned pale. "You think that could happen to us?"

"Nah." Studs shook his head. "I'm working on a structural integrity scan for us." He went on to explain the scanner to Myron, who probably understood none of it but tried to act as if he did.

If Studs had not been working on his ship's integrity scans during the Denebian attack, he told Myron, the whole spacecraft he was on would have been destroyed.

"Yep, we've learned our lesson the hard way not to underestimate the Denebians," he finally said.

After a while Myron abruptly said, "You know, Studs, I get tired of just being a grunt sometimes."

Studs grinned at his helper. "What do you want to be? Captain? Take over from Captain Edge?"

"Well, maybe not captain, but maybe we could be a little bit more than just housecleaners."

Studs slapped his helper on the back. "We'll see what we can do, Myron."

For the first time since Myron and he had been talking, Studs glanced back at the rest of the grunts. He saw that they had stopped working and were listening to the conversation.

"You guys wanna go on this mission?" the crew chief barked.

They all nodded their heads in agreement.

"Then get back to work."

***

Mark Edge, the captain of the *Daystar*, was a good-looking man with blue-gray eyes and crisp blond hair. He was quick to admit he had once been almost a space pirate, but he—and others—considered himself a changed man. Now he served as a captain in Galactic Command.

Captain Edge was seated at his desk and looking over a list when all of a sudden the paper was shoved aside and a long red tongue swiped across his face.

"Contessa, stop that!"

A huge black German shepherd put her paws on Edge's lap and was now trying desperately to lick him. She was a superbred animal, bigger, stronger, and smarter than any others of her breed. She had somehow formed a very warm attachment to Captain Edge, who had always hated dogs.

He tried to shove the animal aside, but she was heavy and he had trouble. "Just get away, Contessa!" he pleaded. "Go find yourself a bone or something!"

"That dog truly loves you, Captain." The speaker was Dr. Temple Cole, the cruiser's medical officer. She was wearing a simple silver uniform with black trim. Her hair was a strawberry color, cut short and very curly. She had enormous violet eyes shadowed by dark lashes. She was so beautiful that the young girls on board were in awe of her—and not a little envious.

Mark pushed at the huge dog until she plopped back on the deck and beat a tattoo with her heavy tail. "You know what they say, Temple. You can always trust a man that a dog trusts."

She smiled but rather sourly. "That's nonsense," she said. "As I've told you many a time, one of the worst men I ever knew had a tremendous attraction to animals. They all loved him, but he'd cut your throat without a moment's hesitation."

"Well, there goes another theory," Edge said. He picked up his list again. "We've got to go through this crew evaluation, so let's get at it."

"I hate that job."

"I do, too, but Commandant Lee says we're overdue with it. Who knows?—maybe some promotions will come out of it."

"You can't get a promotion. You're already the captain."

"Maybe I could get Commandant Lee's job." A slight crinkling appeared at the corners of Mark Edge's eyes, and he grinned. "I think I could run the galaxy as well as she can. After all, she's only a woman," he teased. He knew exactly how Dr. Cole felt about such remarks. "Aw, come on. I'm just kidding," he said. "I'm doing what I want to do. I'll tell you what. Let me make out the report on you." He peeled off a sheet of paper, saying, "Here it is. Dr. Temple Cole. Let's see. I'll say, 'Dr. Cole has performed her duties well. She is competent to set a broken arm or remove splinters. And she is the prettiest doctor in the whole of Intergalactic Command.'"

"You can't send in a report like that!"

"I'll work on it a little bit, then. For now, let's go through the Space Rangers."

They went down the list, commenting on the qualities of the three girls and three boys. Captain Edge saw that, without really trying to, they had put off Heck Jordan until the last. Neither one of them was ever eager to write a report on Jordan. Finally, the captain sighed. "I don't know what to put down about Heck. He's smart and can do anything with computers, but he's a downright pain in the neck most of the time."

28

"I expect a lot of great scientists could be described that way. They're not noted for their easy temperaments."

Still staring down at Heck Jordan's name, Captain Edge shook his head. "I don't see how anyone as big as he is can sneak around and get into so much trouble without being noticed!"

Dr. Cole smiled. "I imagine he's had a lot of practice."

"I've tried to make him lose weight, but he doesn't pay any attention to me. He eats constantly. Maybe he's got some physical problem that makes him eat."

"No. He's just a glutton," the doctor said ruefully. "And any desire to change will have to come from him and not from us."

Captain Edge looked at the dog. Contessa now lay on the floor, her head between her paws. She was fondly looking up at him. She watched every expression of his face and from time to time would nudge his foot with her nose. He reached down and stroked her head. But she got bored with that and, rising from the floor, tried to climb into the captain's lap.

"Oof!" Edge grunted. "Contessa, get down!"

"She just can't help herself. You're so lovable."

"Well, I wish I weren't. She must weigh a ton." He looked at his list one more time. "OK, so what are we going to write about Heck Jordan?"

3

Regent Lansur

Commandant Winona Lee was not impressive look-ing, though she was one of the most powerful women in the galaxy. To the outward eye she was only a small-framed lady of fifty with silver gray hair. She was trimly built and still retained traces of her earlier good looks. But it was in the steadiness of her gray eyes that the force of her mind was revealed.

Pictured on the commandant's viewer was the current ruler of SharNu, Regent Lansur. As the commandant's eyes remained fixed upon the screen before her, she kept her face from showing anything, but in all truth she was disturbed. She wondered, *Is it simply because Lansur is so ugly that I have difficulty talking to him?*

Indeed, Regent Lansur was not an inspiring figure. He was small, no more than five two. His balding head was adorned with only puffs of silver hair that grew randomly. To the commandant, perhaps the most disturbing thing about the regent were his dark, lifeless eyes. *They are much like the eyes of a shark,* she thought. The regent also had skinny arms and legs, and he waved his hands frequently while he spoke in a high-pitched voice.

"Commandant Lee, you are familiar, of course, with our history."

"It's been some time, Regent Lansur, since I heard it. Perhaps you would refresh my memory."

"Of course. You might remember that our queen,

Daleth, was apparently the victim of the White Dragon who dwells in the North Polar Region."

"The White Dragon."

"Yes." The regent nodded, but his cold eyes showed no light whatsoever. "The White Dragon has not been seen by man for many years, but we have reports that it was seen when it carried the queen away."

"I do know of King Regur—that he led a party to rescue her."

Regent Lansur put up his hands in a helpless gesture. "I did all I could to persuade the king, but he would not listen. He refused to believe that his wife was dead. Against my counsel, he gathered his most courageous warriors and set out for the North Polar Region on a rescue mission."

"I honor him for his loyalty to his wife."

But the regent sneered. "Loyalty is one thing, Commandant Lee, but foolishness is another. No man in his right mind would challenge the White Dragon!"

"What became of the king's mission?"

"He was never heard from again, of course. Just as I told him. He was a fool to go."

"You've heard nothing in all this time?"

"No. And it has been twelve years."

"And you have ruled as regent during that time. There is a son, an heir to the throne, I believe?"

"You are correct. Prince Willuin is now approaching his sixteenth birthday. According to our law," Regent Lansur went on, "it is the custom on SharNu for the prince to be crowned king on that day."

"So Prince Willuin will rule?"

"Exactly. That is why I have communicated with you. The prince will be honored by a celebration upon reaching sixteen. He will be crowned king at the Royal Palace of the Ancients in exactly three weeks."

Commandant Lee was always thinking of the politics of situations. She had been commanded by her superiors to be certain that good relationships were maintained with the planet SharNu, but for some reason she did not trust the regent. "I would like to meet with the young prince."

The dark eyes of the regent showed something at that moment, and his right eyelid flickered. Commandant Lee marked this, for she had learned to read the facial expressions of both her enemies and her friends.

"I'm afraid that will not be possible, Commandant," he said.

"And why not?"

"Commandant Lee, Prince Willuin is kept hidden away for safety concerns at the king's secret fortress, Draconia."

"Draconia. A most interesting name. And where is that?"

"The ancients of SharNu named the fortress in honor of the White Dragon. It is secluded deep in the Sylvan Timberlands. So secluded, in fact, that many persons have simply disappeared in this forest, trying to reach it."

"Why would they have disappeared? What happened to them?"

"Some think that the forest may be visited by the White Dragon from time to time. I am not certain of that, but I do know that mysteries abound in the Timberlands. I have been there myself, Commandant, and I have heard the voices of people talking in the forest when there was no one to talk."

Commandant Lee had to restrain herself. "Have you ever seen the White Dragon yourself, Regent Lansur? Do you know of any living person who has seen it?"

"Actually, no."

"Then how can one be sure that there is such an unlikely creature? It seems that you have only vague reports . . ."

"You don't have to see the White Dragon, Commandant, to believe in it!" The man's voice crackled with anger as he replied. "I have seen the destruction that the beast leaves behind. Whole villages are burned to the ground. As I said, people disappear without a trace. Oh, the White Dragon exists, all right!"

Lee said forcefully, "However, sir, my superiors have instructed me to communicate directly with the prince. I must insist on that, Regent."

"I regret that I cannot comply with your request," the regent said firmly. "The prince has been hidden away for these many years. I myself communicate with him only by special courier."

Commandant Lee did not feel that she could press the matter any further. She stared at the regent's face a moment, then changed the subject. "And what is it that you are asking of Intergalactic Command, Regent Lansur?"

"I would like to extend an invitation for Intergalactic Command to send representatives to Prince Willuin's coronation."

Lee at once understood his thinking—and the thinking of her superiors as well. SharNu was an important planet and could play a vital role in future galactic affairs. Since that was so, it would be good politics for Intergalactic Command to become involved with the leadership of the planet. "I can happily agree to that, Regent Lansur. You may expect our representatives very soon."

"Thank you, Commandant Lee. We will look forward to a long and happy relationship with Intergalactic Command."

The screen flickered and went blank. Commandant Lee sat thinking. She considered several of her officers whom she might send as representatives. One by one, she discarded them. Finally a smile touched her lips, and a hint of humor came into her gray eyes. "I believe I'll send the *Daystar*. Regent Lansur is a slippery and clever man, but I don't think he will be concerned over youngsters like the Space Rangers. He will never suspect they are gathering information."

"Heck," Jerusha Ericson cried, "you just must understand that teamwork is everything on a starship!"

Heck Jordan popped a red jellybean into his mouth. He always went through and picked out the black ones and ate them first, but they were all gone so he had to be satisfied with what was left. "I don't believe that," he said. "I get more done working by myself."

"That's not true. Why, then, are you always getting Ringo to help you with your wild schemes?"

Heck waved his hand airily, then searched diligently until he found a grape jellybean. He tossed it into his mouth, chewed on it, then answered. "Ringo's just my helper."

Heck and Jerusha kept on arguing while they worked. They were trying to solve a polarity glitch in the antigravity unit he had been working on. The switch that he had chosen was beginning to malfunction. And if the switch malfunctioned while the antigrav unit was operating, things could become very dangerous for the person wearing it.

Suddenly Heck gave Jerusha a sideways glance. He could not imagine any girl—including Jerusha—not being interested in him. The fact that none of them fell over themselves to become friendly never really bothered him. He studied her for a moment, then asked abruptly, "What about you and that fellow Karl Bentlow you were so crazy about?"

"Karl Bentlow? I was never crazy about Karl Bentlow."

"Sure you were. You liked him a lot—a whole lot, if I remember right. You looked at him—how do you say?—goo-goo-eyed."

Jerusha stayed busy with the task at hand. "Karl was a friend. Starship geography doesn't work very well with building boyfriend-girlfriend relationships."

This was true enough, Heck thought. Right now, Jerusha and Karl Bentlow were at opposite ends of the galaxy from each other. He knew that she had not seen him for a long time.

Heck worked and munched on his jellybeans for a while longer. Finally he said, "I kind of liked Olga, though." Olga Von Kemp, who had, along with Karl, survived a hair-raising adventure with Sir Richard Irons. "She wasn't pretty enough for me, but I liked her —sort of. Maybe I'll give her a break and look her up when we get back to Earth."

Jerusha seemed to be hardly listening, but he rambled on anyway until at last she said, "Heck Jordan, you need to pay more attention to your work and less attention to your romances. That's what a good space officer would do."

"You mean like Captain Edge? He's not paying you any attention these days, either, is he?"

He saw Jerusha's face cloud over. Everybody on the cruiser knew she'd had a hopeless crush on the captain when she joined the *Daystar* crew. It was clear she did not like to have that mentioned.

"My love life is none of your business, Heck!" she snapped. "Now quiet down, and let's get this job done!"

"When I get rich, you'll feel differently about me than you do right now."

Jerusha got to her feet and walked away.

"Hey," Heck called after her, "what about all that teamwork you were talking about, Jerusha? Come back here! You're part of our team!"

She looked back from the door. "Heck, no matter how rich you get, I don't see myself ever getting romantically interested in you!"

"Why not? I'll have money, power, position, fame. You name it. The galaxy will become my footstool."

"How could I ever feel much of anything for such a self-centered person?"

As Heck watched Jerusha disappear into the corridor, he laughed. "You'll whistle a different tune someday."

"You will too, Mr. Jordan," she called back from the hall, "when you discover that someone else— someone *really* important—already has his feet on that footstool."

Dai Bando and Tara Jaleel were sparring in the training room. The martial art of Jai-Kando required lightning-fast moves. The loose-fitting white garments they wore enabled their limbs to fly through their routines.

Jaleel was taking her time, Dai thought. She was always looking for his weaknesses. But Dai toyed with her. He simply would not be struck. He eluded her blows as if he were a ghost.

Finally, after launching one attack, Tara Jaleel lost her temper completely. She screamed Masai battle cries and then swore at him, using Shiva curses.

But Dai smiled at her and waited, refusing to be affected by her rage. All he said was, "Why don't we take a break? I could use it." In all truth, he did not need a break. He was not even breathing hard, but he could tell that the weapons officer was nearly exhausted. By now the woman was drenched with sweat and was moving slowly. He walked over to a bench, saying, "Come on, Lieutenant. It's been a hard workout."

Lieutenant Jaleel just slouched against the wall.

Dai looked up at her from the bench and smiled again in friendly fashion. He sensed that the weapons officer was totally frustrated because she had never been able to defeat him.

Something seemed to come over Tara Jaleel in that moment. She stared at him, shaking her head. Finally she said, "I don't understand you. I just don't understand you."

"Why not, Lieutenant Jaleel?"

"I've tried everything I know to smash you to bits, but you still treat me as a friend. Don't you hate me?"

And then Dai saw something that he had never seen before. He had seen hatred in the eyes of Tara Jaleel. He had seen battle fury in her eyes. He had seen her as a woman who lived to fight, and she was indeed a fine weapons officer. But for the first time ever he was seeing a longing in her eyes for something more than battle. That look gave him hope, and he thought, *God is doing something in the lieutenant's heart.*

Thoughtfully, he said, "Lieutenant Jaleel, is knowing the truth important in Jai-Kando?"

"Of course it is!" she said. Then she gave him a long look and added more slowly, "All my life I've believed that Shiva is the truth."

"But now you're not so sure, are you? Not anymore."

Shock seemed to run through Lieutenant Jaleel. She looked down at her hands, and they were trembling. If Shiva had always been the center of her life, was she beginning to wonder if she had put her trust in the wrong place? In any case, perhaps she did not want him to see that she was shaken, for she reached for a towel, put it around her neck, and walked off, saying, "I don't have time for any more practice today."

Dai Bando bowed his head and smiled. "Lord," he said, "You're on her trail. Don't let her get away. She sure does need a touch from the living God!"

4

The Commandant's Orders

The captain of the *Daystar* sat before the monitor in his quarters and studied the face of his superior, Commandant Lee. Captain Edge was always impressed by her firm attitude, and long ago he had resolved never to do anything that would bring down her wrath on his head. It was perhaps strange for a tall, strong ex-space pirate to be somewhat afraid of a little gray-haired lady, but Commandant Lee wielded great power in the galaxy. The captain listened carefully now as she explained the situation.

"And so I think it would be good if you have Mei-Lani give you a close overview of the history of SharNu. There still may be things we do not understand, but at least you will have some background."

"Can you just give me the overall picture, Commandant?"

"Basically it is this. King Regur disappeared some years ago. His wife had been taken off by a white dragon —or so he believed. He was searching for her."

"A what? Do dragons even exist?"

Commandant Lee smiled briefly. "That was exactly what I thought, Captain, when I heard the story from the regent, Lansur. But whether they do exist or not, one thing is certain. The king and the queen did both disappear, leaving Prince Willuin as a four-year-old child."

"And this Regent Lansur, I take it that he has ruled the country ever since."

"Yes, he has." There was a brief hesitation, and

then Commandant Lee said, "You must be very careful with this, Mark. We must not upset the balance of politics in this sector. The regent rules the planet, and we must not cross him. Be extracareful."

Edge rubbed his chin thoughtfully and studied the woman's image on the screen. "I also take it that you don't have complete confidence in Lansur, Commandant?"

"I do not."

"Woman's intuition?"

Lee gave him a withering look. "I have learned a great deal about people in my long years, Captain Edge. I would not call it woman's intuition but rather wisdom."

"Oh, I'm sure of that, Commandant! But now, what are *Daystar*'s instructions?"

"The crown prince, Willuin, will arrive at the age to rule in a few weeks. The regent has prepared an impressive ceremony and a celebration for the prince's sixteenth birthday. Intergalactic Command has been invited—probably as a mere matter of courtesy. At least that was the feeling I got when Lansur gave me the invitation. You and the Space Rangers will attend as my representatives."

"And what part do you mean the *Daystar* to play in this celebration?"

"My feeling is that Regent Lansur is up to no good, Mark. Somehow I feel that the man is dangerously ambitious, and it is obvious that only one young man stands in the way of Lansur's becoming the permanent ruler over SharNu."

"I see. You're afraid that he might take out the prince?"

Again the commandant paused. She ran a hand over her gray hair and seemed to be thinking deeply.

"My contacts on the planet have informed me that strange things have been happening there. As a matter of fact, all of my contacts on SharNu—except one—have strangely and mysteriously disappeared. That alone is enough to make me suspicious. Something is going on. Something not good."

"Who is your remaining contact? Is he someone you can trust?"

Lee smiled in amusement. "Why do you say *he*? Must it be a man?"

Edge grinned ruefully and shook his head. "Certainly not, Commandant. I just assumed—"

"The contact person is a woman. Her name is Gina Boyd, and she works as a guide for those crossing the Sylvan Timberlands. Her home is located there in a city called Ingara."

"Is she an older woman or what?"

"She actually is very young but very wise. Don't underestimate her abilities—sometimes you find old heads inside young bodies. She is highly capable. In a sense you'll be putting your safety and the safety of your ship in her hands, but Gina Boyd is one you can trust."

Mark Edge nodded and listened until the face of the Commandant faded away. Then he leaned back in his chair, locked his hands behind his head, and frowned. "So we've got to go to a strange planet and protect a prince, a mere boy, from an evil ruler, and everything depends on trusting a very young woman. Just what I like!"

The palace on SharNu seemed to be much like the ancient castles of Earth's history, where the residence of the king was built to display wealth and splendor. Everywhere one looked were paintings of dragons, statues of dragons, and reliefs of dragons built into the palace walls. There wasn't a place in the castle that was without a dragon's image. One could safely call it "The Castle of Dragons."

Seated about a long table in the council chamber —an impressive room with a high ceiling—were twelve men. The Council of Twelve they were called. These men were the official cabinet officers of the planet, and all of them were older men. Some looked to be very old indeed.

The elder of the council, the most powerful member, was a tall, silver-haired man named Murrin. He leaned back in his chair and patiently listened to the talk that ran around the table. But at the same time he was studying the faces of the other council members. He saw that most of them showed traces of agitation, some of outright fear.

And no wonder, Murrin thought. *Most of our council have had family members and friends mysteriously disappear—always after they have disagreed with Lansur. And I do not believe this is any accident.* He glanced at Lansur and, as always, was repelled by the regent's appearance. *I don't trust the man, but I well know what would happen to my sons and my grandchildren if I ever crossed him.*

At that moment Regent Lansur arose. He was very sensitive about his short stature and had had a platform built at his end of the table so that, when standing, he seemed to be rather tall instead of slightly over five feet. He was wearing a purple robe with an insignia of a lightning bolt emblazoned across the chest.

Lansur's cold, emotionless eyes moved around the table for a moment, and then he said, "The council has several decisions to make today. Most important are the coronation plans." He went on to tell them the

44

details of the event. Then, as if it were an afterthought, he said, "The prince will travel by caravan directly across the Sylvan Timberlands to the coronation."

Murrin at once straightened up. He was so shocked that he said in a loud voice, "But, Regent, that area is very dangerous for travel!"

"Don't talk nonsense, Murrin."

Murrin ordinarily would not have argued, but he felt deep concern for the young prince. "Would it not be a simple matter, Regent, to send the prince by air transport? There are untold dangers in a ground journey, as we all know."

At once, other council members began to agree with Murrin, and Regent Lansur's pale face suddenly grew red. His right eyelid flickered uncontrollably, as it always did when he was under stress. He screamed, "I will have quiet in here! *Quiet!* All of you!" He waited until all the council members held their peace, then for a time sat glaring at them. There was something deadly and cold in his eyes. But Murrin—and the others—well knew that there was a steel will beneath the surface.

Lansur pinned them all with his gaze, one by one, as he went on. "The coronation will proceed exactly as I have outlined it. It will be a test of Prince Willuin's maturity. Sooner or later he will have to face dangers as king of SharNu. He will have responsibilities. It is time that he is put to the test. There will be no more discussion on this matter." He waited, and his eyes seemed particularly fixed on Murrin.

The elder of the council knew that he was in a helpless position. "Let it be as you say, Regent Lansur," he said heavily.

From their position on the bridge, Captain Edge, Navigator Llewellen, and First Officer Thrax looked out the portal into space and watched SharNu orbit around its star Eltanin. What they saw was surely as unusual an orbit as Edge had ever seen. The planet seemed to spin at a ninety-degree angle to the sun, so that the southern hemisphere was always pointed toward the light and the northern hemisphere was always in darkness. SharNu was a planet that knew no seasons. How this could happen was a mystery to Galactic Command.

The part of the planet that directly faced the sun was one huge desert that appeared as hot and dry as Mercury. Certainly that cracked, parched land would not be hospitable to any kind of life. On the opposite side of SharNu was the exact opposite environmental extreme. Ice extended from the center of the planet all the way to the pole. At the point farthest from the sun, a huge thick cloud covered several mountain ranges. The wind pummeled the cloud, making it churn about in surreal movements.

Only a thin belt of land between the desert and the ice was able to support life. For the most part, this belt was dominated by a vast dense forest. The sand color of the south, the lush green belt in the center, and the ice-cold white of the north was striking.

What concerned Captain Edge was that there were no spaceports on SharNu. They would have to find a large flat area in order to set down the *Daystar.*

Zeno Thrax, at his side, looked out the portal anxiously. The first officer's skin was always pale, his eyes were colorless, and his hair was pure white, though he was not an old man. Thrax came from Mentor Seven where everyone lived underground, and to be out in space usually gave him a sense of homesickness. He became lonely for the dark tunnels and caverns where he had lived throughout his childhood.

When Captain Edge finished describing their newly assigned mission, Thrax turned abruptly to Bronwen Llewellen.

"Do you believe in dragons, Navigator?"

Bronwen smiled. "Do you, Mr. Thrax?"

"No. I've always thought they were just creatures in a myth."

"That's what I thought myself," Captain Edge said. "But the people on SharNu seem to believe in them—based on some long-ago evidence, apparently."

Bronwen said quietly, "I know there are ancient legends of space dragons in this sector of space. Giant space-faring white dragons were supposed to have migrated to the different planets in the Draco constellation."

"Did anybody ever take a picture of one?" Edge grinned.

"You're not very romantic, Captain."

"Not a bit. I like evidence. Hard facts. No legends. Just one photograph of a space dragon might convince me—even though that itself could be faked. Back on Earth, years ago, many people believed that there was a sea monster living in Loch Ness in Scotland. No one ever actually saw the thing, but people made pilgrimages just in the hope they'd get to see it. I suspect that these white dragons are in the Loch Ness monster category."

"Well, for whatever reason, you will find that the people of SharNu have great faith in the white dragons, Captain."

Edge chewed his lip thoughtfully. Then he said, "I don't know why, but somehow I feel that young Prince Willuin is in danger. I doubt that Commandant Lee sent us on this journey just to look for mythological dragons. If the prince *is* in danger, it's not from a dragon.

His enemy has two feet and doesn't breathe fire, but he's very dangerous just the same."

"Is there a photograph of the prince, Bronwen?" Zeno asked.

"I've searched the files, but the only picture on file was taken when he was only four years old."

A gleam of humor appeared in Thrax's pale eyes. "However, we'll certainly be able to recognize the prince when we see him."

"How do you propose to do that? The picture was taken when he was four, and now he's almost sixteen!"

Thrax grinned broadly now. "Prince Willuin will probably be the only one wearing a crown."

The navigator giggled, and Captain Edge had to grin, himself. "You're probably right, Zeno. Find the person wearing a crown, and we're all right."

5
Two Plans

Zeno Thrax had always said that when three girls got together there would be giggling, whatever else might happen. Jerusha had to admit that the first officer's observation was usually true as far as the feminine side of the *Daystar* Space Rangers was concerned. Jerusha, Mei-Lani, and Raina might be far out in space, but at times they behaved exactly as girls have always behaved at a sleepover or pool party.

The three girls had been drawn very close by their adventures on the *Daystar*. They had traveled throughout the galaxy and faced danger together. This afternoon they were all off duty, and from Mei-Lani's quarters the sound of laughter issued forth. Those passing by caught the sound of it and had to smile.

Mei-Lani's quarters were unusual. She had mementos on her shelves and hangings on the walls that suggested oriental gardens. She was sitting at her computer when Jerusha and Raina entered and sprawled on the soft animal-skin rug.

"What are you doing, Mei-Lani?" Jerusha asked. "Take a break."

"I thought I'd just find out all I could about SharNu before we got there. My parents went to SharNu once, you know."

Mei-Lani Lao's father and mother had both been famous galactic archeologists. They had perished during one of their distant expeditions.

Raina and Jerusha chattered away happily.

49

Mei-Lani continued to listen and work on the screen at the same time until Raina finally said, "I'm thirsty—and hungry too! Let's go down to the mess hall for a snack."

"No need to go anywhere. Passion fruit is on its way," Mei-Lani said, jumping up. "Right here." And she brought out the chilled drink.

As they consumed the delicious juice, Jerusha abruptly announced, "When we get to SharNu, we ought to go shopping and buy some new clothes."

"Are you sure you want to do that? How do you know what they wear on SharNu? The girls might all wear overalls!" Raina smiled.

"I don't care what they wear," Jerusha said. "I'm going to buy a nice looking outfit. I haven't had any new clothes in I don't know how long. I'm going to get a lime green outfit with purple trim."

Raina held her head. "You'll look as bad as Heck," she said. "He looks like a walking rainbow sometimes, when his colors don't match."

"Well, I like purple, and I like lime green, and I'm going to go looking for an outfit. They must have *some* stores on SharNu. After all—" she winked at Mei-Lani "—we may meet some good-looking boys. You never know."

Mei-Lani laughed out loud. "I knew it would come to that sooner or later."

The three girls jabbered and giggled and drank juice, and then Mei-Lani began talking about their mission on SharNu. "I've been trying to get information on the prince, but I can't find a single picture of him in the data banks—except that one when he was four years old."

"Prince Willuin," Jerusha said dreamily. "I'll bet he's tall and dark and handsome."

"He could be short and ugly," Raina teased.

"Well, whatever he looks like," Mei-Lani put in, "he sounds like a fine person from the computer report I pulled up."

"Well, anyway, I'm hoping he's cute," Jerusha said. Then she asked curiously, "You don't really believe in those white dragon stories, do you, Mei-Lani?"

Mei-Lani's face grew thoughtful. "My parents really thought they were more than just myth."

"They did? But they were scientists."

"I know. But they believed there truly had been dragons on SharNu at one time. They thought there were none still in existence—at least none that they could find. Dragons all seemed to have disappeared from the planet a long time ago—sort of like Earth's dinosaurs. But once there had been real dragons."

The talk about dragons went on for a while until Jerusha finally shrugged her shoulders. "Oh, well. When we get to SharNu, I'm still going to buy something to wear. Whenever I get restless, I always like to go shopping. It soothes my nerves. Let's go just as soon as the *Daystar* lands on the planet."

In the Engineering section of *Daystar*, Captain Edge faced a small group that included Tara Jaleel, Studs Cagney, and the grunts who did the actual hard work of the spaceship. He was just finishing telling them about King Regur's ill-fated expedition. "From what I can gather, the king was headed toward the highest mountain deep inside the North Polar Region. That entire mountain range is always covered by a thick cloud and—"

"What kind of a cloud?" Tara Jaleel interrupted, her dark eyes filled with interest. "A volcanic cloud?"

"I am not sure what kind it is, but they call it the Cloud of Unknowing."

"What kind of a name is that for a cloud?" Studs broke in. "The Cloud of Unknowing!"

"Yeah. Why do they call it that?" Myron, Studs's chief grunt, asked.

"Because as far as I can understand, once a person enters the mountains and gets into this cloud, he's just never heard of again."

Myron said quickly, "Probably be a good idea not to go near there."

"Forget it, Myron!" Studs said. He looked back at the captain. "So what's the plan, sir?"

"Basically here's what will happen," Mark Edge said, turning to the viewer. "In the time before the prince's coronation, we'll all do a little investigating. First, you'll drop off Bronwen and the Space Rangers and me in Ingara, the capital city. Thrax will set down the *Daystar* close to the cloud covering the highest mountain—right here. Get out and take a look around, but stay away from that cloud! The rest of us will have a look around Ingara—that's where the king's expedition began."

"What are we looking for?" the weapons officer asked.

"Any trace of the king. Find out where he was seen. Who talked to him last. Was he really heading for the dominant mountain, as I'm guessing he was. Maybe he left a message with someone . . ."

"Sounds to me that'll be like looking for a needle in a haystack!" Studs mumbled.

"You'd better stay in contact with the *Daystar*—in case you need help," the weapons officer warned him.

"That's exactly what will happen, Lieutenant Jaleel. Now, are we straight on all this?"

Myron looked around at the other grunts. Then he said, "Captain Edge, I want to thank you very much for letting us take part in this mission."

Edge shook his hand firmly, but he said with a smile, "Better wait to thank me until after the mission, Myron. Where you're going will be colder than you can ever believe."

Now Tara Jaleel was scowling. "These grunts are not trained for this kind of situation, Captain. They're just not ready."

"Sure they are," Studs argued. He did all the training of the grunts himself and was always very proud of them. "They've been practicing with Dai Bando, and they're ready for new responsibilities."

Edge listened to Tara Jaleel argue against using the grunts, but he still said firmly, "I have decided to use the grunts."

The weapons officer looked very unhappy, but the grunts cheered as the captain started for the door.

Then Edge had an afterthought, and he turned back at the doorway. "Oh yes," he said, "I should mention that Heck Jordan will be going with you."

A groan went up, and all the happy faces turned sour.

"I'm sure you'll enjoy Heck's company." The captain grinned crookedly and again turned to leave Engineering. "At least I won't have to worry about Heck Jordan getting into trouble if he's off somewhere next to the Cloud of Unknowing."

Starting down the corridor, he thought, *Maybe the frigid cold will slow him down a bit.*

Regent Lansur leaned forward to better study the face of the man he had summoned. Balin the bandit was a thick-bodied, muscular man with a brutal face and small yellowish eyes. *He certainly looks villain-ous enough to do anything that needs doing*, the regent thought. Then he spoke aloud. "This is your chance to be rich, Balin, you and your companions."

The bandit smiled, showing crooked yellow teeth. "Make me rich, and I'll do anything. What is it you want? Somebody killed?"

"Enough of that talk. These walls have ears."

Balin shrugged. "It's your place, isn't it? And I'm sure you didn't send for me and my men to have a tea party. What is it you want done?"

Lansur nodded toward the balcony. "What you do and what we say about it are two different things, Balin," he said when they were out where they could talk safely. "Now, let me tell you what you are to do. You know the prince is going to travel from the fortress Draconia through the Sylvan Timberlands to the Royal Palace of the Ancients . . ."

Balin listened as the regent went on to speak of the coronation plans. Once the bandit interrupted to ask, "But what's all this got to do with me and my men? The prince is going to a coronation. So what?"

"You're an impatient fellow, Balin. Here is what will happen." Lansur leaned forward again. This time he whispered, even though the two were alone on the balcony. "I want everyone in that caravan to totally disappear. However you can manage it."

Even Balin appeared somewhat shocked. "You mean the prince too?"

"I mean *especially* the prince! Do you understand me? They must all be done away with—without a trace. They must never reach the Palace of the Ancients. I want you to burn the caravan and every-thing in it—to cinders."

Balin's grin was broad. "And that will put you in a

good position, won't it, Regent Lansur?" he asked shrewdly. "No king. No heirs. Nobody to rule—except you."

"You just do your job, Balin!" the regent snapped.

"Let's talk about money. What's all this job worth to you?"

Lansur said, "Twenty thousand crotas."

"Forty," Balin said.

They argued for a while but finally agreed on a compromise. Lansur went back inside for a moneybag. When he returned, he began to count out half of the payment.

Balin seemed to enjoy the sound of the gold coins clinking together. He dropped them into his own money bag and said, "I'll be back for the rest when the job is done."

"Once I'm king, Balin," the regent promised, "you'll have riches beyond your wildest dreams. I'll need men like you to keep this planet exactly where I want it."

Balin laughed this time. The gold coins jingled in their leather sack as he left.

Lansur watched him go, then pushed a button on his desk. At once, his second in command came in. Masa was a lean individual with hollow cheeks and watchful gray eyes. "How did it go?" he asked.

"It went all right. Balin will take care of the caravan, and that will be the end of all the royal family."

"Still, in a sense you have put yourself in the power of Balin, have you not? He knows you are responsible. If he tells . . ."

Regent Lansur squinted thoughtfully at his second officer. "Masa, after the caravan disappears, it would not surprise me if Balin and his whole team wound up being dragon food."

"That is one way to keep him quiet, indeed," Masa said.

The regent and his aide laughed together.

Then Lansur said, "Things are going well. Nothing can stop us now."

6
The Strange Crystal

The *Daystar* flew out of deep space and made a perfect landing on a great flat knoll just outside the city of Ingara. A high wall containing fourteen gates encircled the town. Computer data said that the capital of the planet was densely populated. That wall was needed for protection from the fierce animals that roamed the forest region.

Captain Edge called the entire crew together and gave his orders crisply. "Bronwen and I will have to meet with the regent, but first I intend to go and find Commandant Lee's contact here. I want most of the Rangers to go with me into Ingara." He did not tell them yet, but his plan was to eventually get to the fortress Draconia and join the prince's caravan.

Jerusha's face brightened at once. "Captain Edge, would we have time to do some shopping?"

"Shopping! You're on an important mission!" Edge protested.

"But, Captain," Jerusha pleaded, "we have to look presentable, don't we?"

"I suppose so," the captain growled. "All right. All right. You can go shopping. In fact, maybe it's a good idea. You'll blend in a little better if you dress as the natives do."

He heard Heck Jordan groan and mutter to Ringo, "I can't stand it." Then he turned brightly to Captain Edge. "Captain," he said, "Ringo and I need to go into town and do some shopping, too. We can buy ourselves some nice clothes, and then we'll be right in style—just like the girls." With that, he suddenly reached over and tapped Jerusha on the shoulder.

Something in Heck's voice or action must have irritated the dog, Contessa. Jerusha's giant German shepherd was very protective of her mistress, and she had never liked Heck much to begin with. The dog was up in a flash. She made a flying leap and knocked Heck flat on his back. She planted her paws on his chest, and her white fangs showed as she growled deep in her throat.

"Get this monster off of me, Jerusha!"

"We ought to let her eat you," Captain Edge said. "Then we'd be rid of a lot of trouble." He walked to where the German shepherd was keeping Heck Jordan pinned to the deck and placed a hand on the dog's neck. "All right, Contessa. Let him up."

Reluctantly Contessa moved back, but she kept watching Heck just the same.

Captain Edge pulled Heck to his feet and inspected his outfit from head to foot. Heck was off duty, so he was not wearing his uniform, which was rather attractive. Instead, he had on a pair of red trousers, a brilliant orange shirt, and a rather sickly green neckerchief.

"You don't have to worry about what you're going to wear to be in style, Heck. You'll be wearing an envirosuit."

"An envirosuit! What for?" Heck protested.

"Because you're going with the grunts to the North Polar Region, and I hope it freezes some sense into you."

A giggle went up from the girls, and Mei-Lani said, "Bring me back some ice to make ice cream, Heck."

Heck glared at her and then looked angrily around at everyone else.

Dai Bando must have felt sorry for Heck. Dai was always a very warmhearted boy anyway. He walked over and put a hand on Heck's shoulder.

"I'll go with you, Heck," he offered with a smile. "If the captain will let me, that is. We might have ourselves a good time in the North Polar Region."

"Sorry, Dai. I've got something else I want you to do," Captain Edge told him. "The grunts can protect Heck."

Now Heck glared at the captain. "I don't need anybody's protection!" he said loudly. "I can take care of myself!"

Edge said, "Yes, I've seen how you take care of yourself." Then he turned to the group as a whole. "After the navigator and the other Rangers and I leave for Ingara, Thrax and Ivan will fly the rest of you to the North Polar Region. Now, it's your job there to try to find some trace of the king. He disappeared in that area, and we're hoping he might have left some clue, perhaps even a message written down."

"If he did, I'll find it," Heck declared. "I could find a needle in a haystack."

Captain Edge ignored this. "Bronwen," he said, "I want you to go to the palace at once and meet with the regent. You'll be an official representative from Galactic Command. Now be careful. We don't know much about this Regent Lansur, but don't believe anything he says and keep your eye open for anything that looks suspicious."

Mei-Lani thought that Ingara was an interesting city with its narrow streets and vendors hawking wares in every direction. And she noticed the curious eyes that followed Captain Edge and the Space Rangers wherever they went.

At the business place of Gina Boyd, the group went inside and looked around curiously. It was a shop. There were blue crystals on display and artifacts that Miss Boyd had discovered in the forest. Most people were too scared to travel in the forest, she told them, and that made her finds worth even more. Many seedy looking people roamed about in her store, maybe hoping to find a good bargain.

As for Gina Boyd herself, she was a very attractive young lady. *She must be twenty or twenty-one*, Mei-Lani guessed. The girl was of medium height with long brunette hair, and she had green eyes that sparkled when she laughed. She looked like the strong, athletic type. As the captain spoke with her, Mei-Lani could tell that she also had a very quick mind.

"Commandant Lee said you could help us," Captain Edge said. "We need to join up with Prince Willuin, and I understand you know the Sylvan Timberlands."

"I know that area better than anybody else," she said, and it did not sound like boasting. "Here. Let me show you a map. The prince's caravan is scheduled to leave the fortress in just a few days."

While Mei-Lani was listening to the conversation, something on a shelf suddenly caught her eye. It was a blue crystal that had some kind of engraving on its front face. She picked up the piece and studied it. It was translucent, and, holding it up, she could look through it. It gave her a rather warped view of the shop. Everything had an unusual appearance as she stared through it.

"What is this, Gina?"

Gina Boyd took a look at the crystal. "Oh, nothing special. Just a blue crystal. They are quite common around Ingara."

"What's this writing on it, though? I'm very interested in languages."

"Actually, no one knows. It's just writing that appears on some crystals. Some people believe the Ancients left it, but I don't think so. Most people use such crystals as good luck charms." Gina smiled and added, "I tend to think a person makes his or her own luck."

Jerusha smiled, too, and said in a friendly way, "And I really don't believe in luck. I think it's God who determines a person's steps."

This time the girl laughed aloud. "All right. Let's see." She looked up and said in a loud voice, "God, tell me what is the next step I should take?" She looked around in the silence and smiled brightly. "See? That proves I'm right. I didn't hear any voice."

Jerusha shook her head. "Maybe that only means that you're not ready to hear God's voice yet."

Gina Boyd considered Jerusha a moment, then shrugged her shoulders. In a sarcastic tone, she said, "Well, thanks a lot, Captain Edge, for bringing me a religious nut!"

Edge said nothing. Everyone else was silent, too, and Gina Boyd began to appear uncomfortable. She stopped smiling. She walked over to Jerusha and put a hand on the girl's shoulder. "That's all right. A wise man once said that if any two people think exactly the same way, one of them isn't thinking."

"I've heard that before," Jerusha said. "And I agree with it as far as human beings are concerned." She looked at the older girl with a very direct gaze. "But God wants us to look at life from His point of view."

Gina looked thoughtful, then said, "Commandant Lee has been trying to tell me the same thing. Well, maybe there's something to it. We'll see."

During this entire conversation, Mei-Lani had been holding the blue crystal. Lifting it up from time to time, she would gaze through it. The piece gave her an odd feeling, and somehow she knew deep within herself that this crystal was very important. She did not know why she felt this way, but the feeling was so strong that she said, "Gina, could I buy this crystal?"

"Keep it, Mei-Lani. It's a gift from me."

"Thank you very much!" Mei-Lani slipped the crystal into her bag and then stood listening as plans were made for the Rangers to join the prince.

Bronwen Llewellen had served in Galactic Command for many years. She had visited many planets and was very much aware of the importance of ceremonies. Now she looked around at the Royal Palace of the Ancients and was impressed by what she saw. The heavy meeting-hall furniture had legs that resembled dragons' legs. Many different flags, all bearing images of dragons, surrounded the perimeter of the hall. One flag was larger than any other. This flag displayed the White Dragon, an animal larger than all the others.

Then the regent was saying, "We are glad to receive you as our honored guest, Lieutenant Llewellen. But now, come. You must enjoy some of our food."

The dining area was alive with pleasant aromas, and Bronwen found the food to be delicious. She ate lightly but did take along a piece of SharNu fruit when, at the close of the dinner, Regent Lansur invited her to go for a walk in the palace gardens.

"You will be impressed, I am sure, Lieutenant, by the upcoming celebration. It will be quite colorful."

The regent went on to describe the ceremonies of the coronation, but Bronwen was listening for something more than this. She had a sense of discernment, and she perceived that something in this man was not right. He reminded her of a tune that was sung almost on key but not quite. It was enough to set her teeth on edge. Her instincts screamed out that this was an insincere man. She had already been warned by the captain to be careful, and now she was doubly so.

When they returned to the palace, Lansur waved a hand, and his second in command—Masa, he said— and an attendant stepped forward. Masa was smaller even than the regent. He had very short dark hair and was clean-shaven. He also had a long, pointed nose, a sly smile, and teeth that made him look somewhat like a weasel. He was dressed in a dark robe. And now he bowed deeply before Bronwen.

The attendant beside Masa wore a scarlet uniform. On his head was a tall hat made of dark animal fur and strapped under his chin.

Lansur spoke to the attendant. "Show the lieutenant to her quarters."

"I would really prefer not to stay at the palace, Regent!" Bronwen cried.

"Oh, but I insist!" And Lansur did insist—so strongly that Bronwen felt she could not refuse. She did not want to offend the man, for his good will was necessary. Bronwen agreed.

Lansur waited until Bronwen Llewellen was out of earshot. Then he said, "Masa, keep a close eye on that woman while she's at the palace. She's a clever one. I don't want her running loose."

"I assure you she will not run loose, Regent."

The regent smiled. Things were going well. Indeed, they could not be better. "It's only a matter of time until the crown is on my head."

"Long live the king." Masa grinned an evil grin.

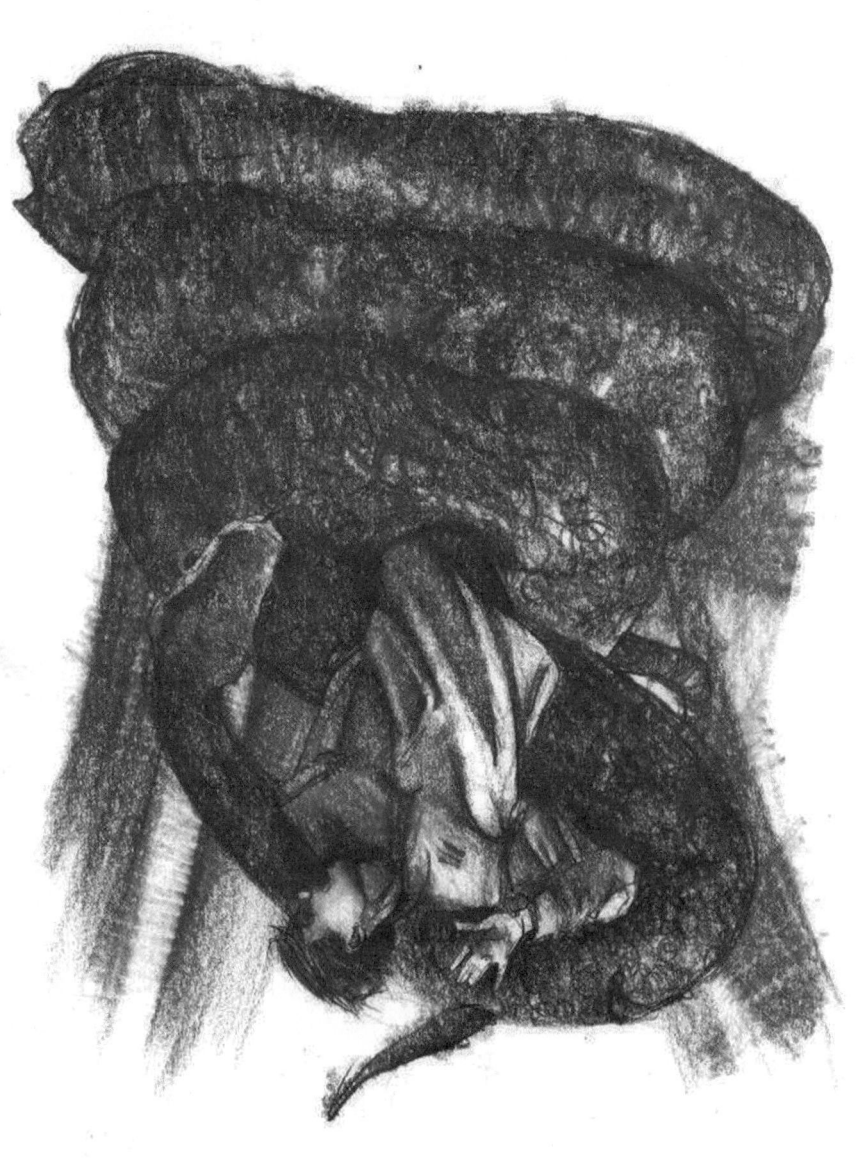

7

The Snake

Prince Willuin even looked much like a prince. He had blond hair, a rosy fair complexion, and a contagious smile. Although rather slender, he was athletic appearing. All of his people knew him as a young man of charm and of great integrity. They also knew that he was a follower of Jesus—although he himself was rather quiet about his faith. People said that he would be a good king. And practically the whole kingdom yearned for the time when he would sit on the throne instead of Regent Lansur.

The king's special jungle fortress was an impressive stronghold indeed. Three large pyramids lifted the stronghold a couple of hundred feet off the forest floor and supported its foundation. As one walked by the pyramids and then looked up at the fortress base, great dragons' heads sprang into view, as if they were slithering out of the fortress through holes in the floor.

At the large front window of the fortress, Willuin stood talking with his three bodyguards, Vav, Yod, and Kaph.

The three had been well chosen to keep their prince safe. They were all unusually tall young men, and the tallest, towering at six feet eight inches, was Vav. He had a large nose and full lips and was very muscular. He was even-tempered, and Willuin thought he had a great deal of common sense.

Standing beside Vav was Yod, only six feet five. He

had long red hair. He could run like a deer and was especially strong.

The third member of the trio, Kaph, had almost black eyes and a mustache that was groomed into a straight line. He had more scars on his body than anyone else the prince had ever known. These came from taking part in many battles.

Prince Willuin was fond of all three of his young friends. He knew they would lay down their lives in a moment for him. So he was listening thoughtfully as Kaph said, "I am very much opposed to this trip, prince."

"Why is that, Kaph?" the prince asked.

"I truly don't know. It's a . . . a feeling I have. It just seems that there's something wrong with this journey."

"Oh, you're always having feelings." But Willuin smiled. "Obviously, we must be prepared for trouble, but we must not *look* as if we were preparing for trouble."

Yod grinned and swung around so suddenly that his long red hair flew out. "You mean," he said, "that you want us to worry, but you want us to look as if we don't have a care in the world."

"That's about it," the prince said cheerfully. "It will be a difficult task for you, for we've always shown on our faces what we were. But discretion is the better part of valor in this case."

Vav flexed his hands and gnawed on his lower lip. "I agree with Kaph, though. I too sense that there's something especially dangerous about this journey across the Timberlands."

"It may well be that there's danger," Prince Willuin said. "But we must face it. Now let me tell you what I have planned."

The three bodyguards listened in silence until the prince finished. Then Vav said, "No, I still think that is too dangerous. What I would like you to do is to put on the uniform of a common soldier. We'll find someone who looks like you, prince. He can wear your royal clothing. Then, if anything happens, all will not be lost."

The prince at once shook his head. "I will not sneak to my own coronation," he said quietly. "The people must see that their new ruler has no fear. I will go as myself, and that's all there is to it."

Some argument took place after this, but Prince Willuin was totally unmovable on this point.

Finally, the three gave up trying to persuade him.

Kaph said with a shrug of his muscular shoulders, "Very well, we will put ourselves in the hands of God."

"There is no better place to be," Prince Willuin said, "than in the hands of the wise and good God."

The *Daystar* prepared to land in the North Polar Region quite near the Cloud of Unknowing. The mountains here were as cold and shear looking as any the crew had ever seen. Only the whiteness of the frozen landscape made vision possible. The entire scene was eerie and spoke of danger. It was clear that no one would long survive this harsh climate without an envirosuit.

Tara Jaleel was especially uncomfortable. Tara hated cold weather. She much preferred the heat of the tropical climates. She shivered even now as the sensors scanned the area. "I despise cold weather," she said aloud. "The cold goes right to my bones."

"It won't bother you after you put on your envirosuit," Zeno Thrax told her. "You won't even know you're in cold weather."

"I won't wear that cumbersome thing! It slows me down too much. How can I fight when I'm wearing a suit like that?"

Thrax grinned. "Look at that temperature gauge."

He pointed, then read the dial aloud. "It's forty degrees below zero. If you don't wear that suit, you'll be slowed down to nothing in two minutes flat. You'd probably freeze into an ice statue."

Thrax guided the cruiser over the mountain range, steadily dropping lower. Suddenly he said, "Look! Right down there. What's that?"

Tara Jaleel looked. "It looks like an old campsite to me."

"I think it is, too, but it's been abandoned for a long time." In an instant, he made up his mind. "This mesa is wide and flat. We'll take the ship in and see what's there."

Hands busy on the controls, Thrax commented, "This could have been a camping place for the king's search party. It's the only sign of human life we've seen." He steered the *Daystar* along the thick cloud toward the campsite.

Abruptly, a warning blast blared.

At once Studs Cagney's voice came over the intercom. "Something just flew over us, sir!"

"What was it?"

"I couldn't see it, but it sure was *something*, and it was something big."

Thrax watched the screen as the *Daystar* completed her descent. "Whatever it was," he said to Lieutenant Jaleel, "there's no indication it was another ship. It must have been something biological."

"But where did it go? I didn't see a thing."

"It could be hidden somewhere among these mountains."

Heck had been standing back listening to the two officers talk. Now he swallowed hard enough to be heard. "I think we ought to abandon this mission," he squeaked.

"Abandon the mission! Are you crazy, Jordan?" Lieutenant Jaleel snapped.

"Well, maybe that was a dragon, and I don't want to be dragon food. I like to eat, but I don't want to be eaten!"

The two officers ignored Heck's protests, and Zeno brought the *Daystar* in for a landing.

Gina Boyd was a fine guide. Knowing this, however, did not make Raina any more comfortable. The jungle was thick, and she could not see into it. This trek was like wading in water up to her chin, with the feeling that at any moment something was going to grab her and bring her down.

Gina Boyd, wearing a loose fitting khaki outfit and hiking boots, had guided Captain Edge and the Space Rangers deep into the Sylvan Timberlands, the official name of the forest belt that girdled SharNu. They would reach the prince's hidden fortress soon—so Gina said.

"I think we're getting lost," Ringo muttered. He looked around at the thick undergrowth, the towering trees, and then at Raina. "It all looks just alike."

Raina felt somewhat the same way. She could not see a single landmark. Finally she caught up with Gina. "Are you sure about this, Gina? I can't tell a thing about the direction we're going."

"It's all right, Raina. I know the way." There was assurance in her voice. She turned around then and viewed the Rangers, straggled out behind her in a ragged line. "Just keep up, all of you! Don't try to think where you are! Just keep up with me!"

She did not say more for some time, and then she turned to Raina, who was still plodding along beside her. "The prince's caravan will travel this same route in just a few days."

Raina looked around at the undergrowth one more time. They had to shove their way through it. She said, "It's all we can do to get through single file. Surely there'll be some kind of a royal procession. So how can—"

"Oh, there will be. But the Path Finders will take care of that."

"Who are the Path Finders? What are they?"

"They are a crew that will cut their way through. They're the best woodsmen that you've ever seen, and they have the equipment to do the job."

Something bothered Raina about that. "But wouldn't that leave a direct path back to the fortress? I thought the fortress was supposed to be kept secret. And besides, people will know exactly where the prince is!"

Gina shook her head and explained as they trudged along. "Not for long. After this undergrowth is cut and there's a path through here, the brush will start growing back. In three or four days, it will be completely grown up again."

"Things grow that fast on SharNu?" Raina could scarcely believe her ears.

"The natives say, 'Get out of the way or you'll be caught in a tree and lifted up to the sky.'"

Ringo was last in the procession, and he didn't like what he saw. In the first place, it was difficult to see the sky, and he felt closed in and cramped. The trees were enormous. They reached up hundreds of feet, and their trunks were thick enough to stun the imagination. They reminded him of the old redwoods on Earth, except that they were much, much larger.

He stopped and lifted his canteen to his lips. It was thirsty work going through the forest. He took several swallows. And then he felt something wrapping itself

70

about his leg! He looked down, and what he saw caused him to drop the canteen. An enormous serpent had emerged from the thicket and was coiling upward about him.

"Help!" Ringo yelled. "Everybody look out! There's snakes here!"

He fought the snake, trying to get free. His efforts were useless. Already the thick reddish serpent was looping itself around his chest. "Help me!" he screamed. "Get this thing off of me!" Then he fell over sideways due to the snake's great weight.

The snake's coils tightened, and Ringo felt his very life being crushed out of him. He tried to take a deep breath to fill his lungs, but they were being pressed flat, as if by a giant vise. He was starting to black out when Gina Boyd leaped into his vision, whacking at the serpent with their one cutting weapon—her machete.

Gina Boyd's great knife slashed. The snake writhed, but now its head was gone.

"Quick! Get these coils off him!" Captain Edge shouted.

The Rangers sprang to help him. Together they dragged away the massive snake.

"He's not breathing!" Raina cried. "He needs oxygen!"

"We don't have anything like that here!" Jerusha cried wildly.

"Out of the way!" Captain Edge ordered. "Let me—"

But without pausing, Raina leaned over Ringo. She parted his lips and placed her mouth over his. She blew as hard as she could and as firmly.

Ringo sensed he had descended into blackness

but now was returning. He did not know where he was, but he felt something very soft on his lips. His eyes came open then, and he realized with a shock that Raina was bending over him. Though his vision was blurred, he knew it was Raina. She always wore a certain perfume. And then he realized that she was bringing him back to life by sharing her breath with him.

Ringo had been attracted to Raina ever since he had met her. He was a very shy boy and not able to express his feelings. But now he knew his time had come. As Raina lifted her head to take a breath, Ringo kissed her on the cheek.

At first Raina blinked. Then she looked angry. Then she stood up. "Ringo Smith, I ought to clobber you!" she said.

Dai helped Ringo to his feet. "You've got to have the biggest smile on your face I've ever seen," he said with a chuckle.

Ringo said, "Well, I just had a dream come true."

Dai laughed and now helped him to walk around.

Raina refused to look at him. Her face was still red with embarrassment.

Gina Boyd watched this, then said, "All right. We've got to move on. *And watch where you're going!*" Her face grew serious, and she shook her head. "There are more dangerous animals in the Sylvan Timberlands than that big snake."

8
The Ice Cave

Bronwen Llewellen tossed and turned restlessly for more than an hour. Her quarters in the palace were certainly pleasant enough. Nevertheless, in spite of the luxurious, comfortable room, she could not sleep.

Rising from the bed, she stretched and lit a lamp. Then she began to walk about, examining the paintings and the statues that abounded in the apartment. Someone must have read a book about ancient England on Earth, for there was a distinct English-castle flavor here. There were even tapestries hanging from the walls that portrayed men with bows and arrows, hunting a stag from horseback.

Bronwen examined the tapestries at length. She loved such things.

Finally, however, she came to a wall that was in shadows. She noted that it was adorned with marble reliefs, though. The marble had been cut away to leave odd-shaped designs that had no artistic quality that she could see. She ran her fingers over the engraved marble for a long time, but the design meant nothing to her.

And then she stepped back from the wall, thinking to look at it from a distance. When she had backed up until she was almost against the opposite wall, Bronwen gasped. She saw that, when viewed from a distance, the meaningless designs formed the head of a terrible dragon. When one stood next to the relief, the dragon's head could not be recognized, but from where she now stood, it was there clearly. She could see the long snout, the scales, the sharp fangs, the forked tongue. Indeed it was very good likeness of a terrible creature.

Curiosity overcame Bronwen. She walked back to stand directly in front of the carved dragon's head. Reaching out a hand, she began to run her fingers over the raised marble relief. As she did so, she heard a slight sound and then received a shock when the mouth of the dragon began to open.

The dragon's mouth grew larger. And larger. And larger. And then Bronwen realized that it was actually a concealed door. She had evidently tripped whatever signal triggered it, and now she stood peering down into darkness. She could see very little, for the passageway that opened before her was almost as black as night.

For some time Bronwen stood wondering what to do. She was an adventurous woman. She always had been. She had been the first woman navigator traveling into deep space, and her courage was noted throughout the galactic world. Besides, she loved a good mystery. So she nodded and said to herself, "I'll never know if I don't try."

She picked up the lamp. Then she stepped into the passageway, thinking with a sudden smile, *This feels like an old novel written in the eighteen hundreds back on Earth.*

She made her way slowly forward until the passage opened into an area where walls and floor and ceiling were all of some dark gray material. She lifted the light higher and looked closely. *They seem to be made of some kind of brick,* she thought.

As Bronwen continued down the gloomy corridor, an occasional torch set in the wall flickered, throwing further shadows over the passage ahead. Had she been a nervous woman, she might have been shaken by this, but she was not.

Her eyes further adjusted to the dimness, and she noted that now there appeared to be doors along the passage and that all of them had barred windows.

"Why, this must be the dungeon of the castle!" she exclaimed aloud. Her voice sounded loud and hollow in the open space, and she walked on more cautiously.

Finally she turned a corner and at once drew up short. Not ten feet away stood Masa, the regent's second in command. A cruel smile was on the man's face. Next to the regent's henchman stood two burly soldiers. Their eyes were fixed on her.

Thinking quickly, Bronwen smiled. "I think I must have gotten lost. I couldn't sleep and was just exploring this beautiful castle, Masa."

When the man did not immediately answer, she continued carefully, "I suppose I can just go back the way I came and find my quarters . . ."

"Seize her!"

The soldiers stepped forward. Each grabbed one of Bronwen's arms. Masa took the lamp from her, and the light threw shadows over his face. He was grinning. "Put her into that cell!" He pointed to the nearest door.

One of the guards took a set of keys from his belt. The door made a rattling, squeaking sound, then a rusty squeal as it opened.

The two men shoved Bronwen into the cell. She fell sprawling, rolled over, and came to her feet. It was a dim, evil smelling place with rank, stale straw on the floor. She heard the door slam and the keys jingle.

Masa laughed aloud then. "Welcome to your new quarters, Bronwen Llewellen. I hope you like them, because you will be here for a very long time."

Ringo looked ahead to where Gina Boyd was pointing. There he could see the fortress, sheltered among the giant trees. "So there it is, Jerusha," he said. "The secret fortress, Draconia."

Jerusha was looking at their guide with admiration. "You did it, Gina! And I think you are very courageous to work so often in a jungle filled with dangerous animals."

When the party reached the fortress entrance, Gina paused at the gate and called up to the tower. "Ho, tower, there! Open the gate!"

"Who calls?"

"Gina Boyd! You know me, fellow! Now open up!"

"Oh yes! We know you well." The guard began to laugh in friendly fashion. "Is there any news?"

"I'm not the town crier, man! Just open the door! Come on. Hurry it up! I've got to get back to Ingara."

Gina Boyd stepped back, and the massive gate began to slide upward.

"A group of mercenaries from Rastaban should have arrived there by now," she yelled to the watchman in the tower. "This is Captain Mark Edge and his party. Take them to see the prince."

"All right, Gina. Will do."

Their guide turned to face the captain. "So now you are here," she said with satisfaction. "I have to go back at once. It's very important. If those mercenaries are who I think they are, they could mean trouble."

"Certainly—you go on, Gina. And thank you. And when you get back to the capital, I wish you'd check on our navigator, Bronwen Llewellen, for me," Edge responded. "Would you do that?"

"Of course, I'll do that."

Their young guide disappeared almost magically into the dense forest, and Edge and the Space Rangers entered Fortress Draconia.

* * *

"Sir, the scanners are picking up a large cavern entrance," Studs Cagney relayed to Zeno Thrax.

"I see it, Studs. I'll maneuver the ship as close as I can."

Skillfully, Thrax settled the *Daystar* quietly not far from the cave opening.

Soon the hatch opened, and First Officer Thrax along with Tara Jaleel, Studs, Heck, Myron, and the rest of the grunts exited the ship. Their envirosuits had been designed to withstand the drastic temperature changes that were found in outer space. The gear therefore was tailor-made for exploring frozen territory. The only people who complained that the suits were uncomfortable were the weapons officer—who did not like to be weighed down by the clumsy outfit—and Heck Jordan, whose own suit fit so tight that the grunts literally had to stretch it over him.

Zeno looked around the campsite and was disappointed. It was old indeed and provided them with no clues. They turned to the cave.

"Go check it out, Jaleel," Zeno said. "Ivan and I will be with the *Daystar* in case you run into a problem. Keep in touch."

The cavern's mammoth entrance was twice the size of the *Daystar.* Inside, its walls were smooth, as if a large blowtorch had melted down the rock.

And as soon as the crew entered, Tara Jaleel saw that the cave floor turned sharply left and started to go downhill. What they had found now appeared to be more a concealed canyon than a true cave.

"I don't know about this," Heck said, peering suspiciously over a ledge into the ravine below. Then he took out his datacorder and scanned the area. "My scans don't pick up anything, but down below there's a really big shelf. It outcrops from the wall about a thousand feet down."

Jaleel, then Studs and the grunts, led the way down the canyon path. If it had not been for their envirosuits, she knew they would have been frozen stiff. Who knew what the temperature was in here? Large ice crystals rose up everywhere.

As she led them deeper and farther down into the canyon, they rounded a turn and suddenly came upon a huge column of gases. It appeared to be funneled from deep in the mountain through a naturally formed chimney. The gas jet was enormous. It shot skyward like an upward flowing waterfall.

"I can't make anything out of that from my scanner," Tara said. "But it looks like the trail keeps on going— right alongside the gas jet and maybe for miles more."

Studs Cagney also had his scanner out. "The gases in that jet are composed partly of hydrogen with small traces of fluorine, chlorine, bromine, iodine, and astatine," he announced. "But most of the gas is halogen."

Everyone turned to gape at him, including Tara Jaleel herself. She never would have suspected that Studs Cagney could know all that.

Studs then added, "It's very unusual to find such a large volume of halogen gas. It usually exists in a free state as diatomic molecules."

That left Myron and most of the other grunts looking totally puzzled. "What does diatomic mean?" Myron asked.

"Oh, you should know that!" Heck said impatiently.

Ignoring Heck, Studs started to answer the question. "A diatomic molecule is a molecule that is made up of just two atoms. *Di* means two—*atomic* means atom. And *molecule* means the little particles of a substance that have all the properties of that substance. It's made up of one or more atoms."

Just as bewildered as before, Myron shook his head, but he thanked Studs anyway.

"Didn't you learn anything in grunt school?" Heck Jordan grumbled at him.

"Quiet, Heck," Tara Jaleel growled, "or I'll throw you off the cliff!"

The rest of the grunts snickered at this. They were generally a good-natured lot who worked very hard. Like Jaleel, they knew Heck was mouthy and know-it-all. They expected such a comment from him.

The party continued downward, and now the pathway grew much steeper. Jaleel warned everybody to hold on to the cliff side, for their feet threatened to slip on the icy spots beneath them. Finally all were standing on the large shelf that everyone had seen from far above.

"And would you look at this!" Studs said in a voice full of wonder.

The others gathered round to see what he had found.

The engineer pointed downward. "See that? Somebody's been here before us."

Tara Jaleel examined Studs's discovery, and without doubt it was the remains of an old campfire. "So it looks like the people from the campsite up above got this far at least."

And then Studs said thoughtfully, "Uh, sir . . . I don't know what it means, sir, but that gas is shooting up pretty fast and . . ."

By now the crew and the grunts all stood staring at the gas as it rose. The gaseous jet seemed to have almost a hypnotic effect.

"Nobody even *look* at that jet anymore!" the weapons officer ordered suddenly.

"What's the matter?" Studs turned to her.

"If somebody got careless and got drawn into that gas jet, he would die from lack of oxygen. Besides—" Jaleel said "—it's time to get moving. We've got to see what we find up ahead. If anything. *And keep your eyes off that gas.*"

9
Meeting in a Dungeon

At first, Bronwen thought her cell was empty. She quickly became aware that it was larger than she had supposed, though. And as her eyes became accustomed to the darkness, which was broken by a single small candle, she was shocked to discover that she had a fellow prisoner.

Bronwen stood very still for a long moment. But when the figure before her did not move or speak, she said, "Hello. I didn't see you at first."

The silence that followed her words echoed in her ears. But there seemed to be no danger, so she moved closer. The light from the candle threw its pale amber glow over the face and the form of a man sitting in a far corner. His long hair and beard concealed his face somewhat, making it impossible to clearly see his features.

Bronwen's eyes finally adjusted to the low light, and she saw that he was so thin that he was almost skeletal. But what impressed her most was his eyes. They had a light in them that she'd come to recognize over the years.

Then she caught a glimpse of something hanging around the man's neck. She leaned toward him, and the object was a medallion. But it was not an ordinary medallion. Her eyes opened wide, and she took in a sharp breath. The medallion around the man's neck was exactly like the medallion that Ringo Smith had worn ever since she had known him. That one had on it the image of Ringo's father, Sir Richard Irons, and Bronwen suddenly burned with curiosity.

"My name is Bronwen Llewellen," she said quietly. "May I know your name?"

For a moment she thought he did not intend to answer, but then he nodded. In a thin, reedy voice he said, "My name is . . . Zayin."

"I would be happy to meet you under more pleasant circumstances," she replied. She waited for him to speak again, and, when he did not, she asked curiously, "Why are you imprisoned here, sir? Have you been here long?"

Again Zayin nodded slowly. "Yes. I have been here for a very long time."

"And what was your crime?"

"I am sure you are not a spy put here to find out secrets, for I have none." A sudden brightening appeared in Zayin's faded eyes, and he said, "You might say I was the instructor of Prince Willuin when he was small. Everything went well until I discovered Lansur's plans—which were to kill the prince when he became king and then rule the planet himself." He added eagerly, "And the prince—does the prince yet live?"

"He does live. Unfortunately, Lansur still acts as regent. But what did you do that brought you here, Zayin?" she asked.

A slight smile came to the bearded man's lips. "I confronted Lansur—a foolish thing to do, for he was powerful even then. He had me thrown into this cell, and I've been here ever since."

"But didn't you have family? Certainly you must have had friends," Bronwen cried. "Why has no one come looking for you? Did no one investigate what had happened?"

Slowly the bearded man shook his head. "You

don't know the evil of Lansur. Friends and family members of those in prison . . . disappear. They are kidnapped—and usually killed—by his henchman Masa. Then the disappearance is blamed on the White Dragon. Actually there is never anything to investigate. Lansur goes to great lengths to deceive. Our people are led to believe that the White Dragon actually exists and feeds itself on humans. Thus the disappearances."

"I have suspected something like this," Bronwen murmured. She reached out suddenly and touched his medallion. "And where did you get this?"

Zayin looked down at the large medal. When he looked at her again, a cautious expression was on his face. "It is an old family keepsake."

Bronwen asked, "May I look at the other side?"

"If you will."

Bronwen turned over the medallion, and, sure enough, on the back was the familiar figure of a falcon. She let it fall back against the man's rags and said, "This medallion is exactly the same as a medallion worn by a boy who is a member of our spaceship crew."

Zayin eyed her suspiciously. "That is hard to believe. This medallion is thousands of years old. I don't even know if there are any more like it anywhere on SharNu."

Bronwen's eyes narrowed, and she sat down beside him. "The boy is not from SharNu, but he has had the medallion nearly all his life. Do you know any of the medallion's history?"

But the bearded prisoner seemed reluctant to give further information. All he would say was, "All I know is that it was made in honor of a great visitor to SharNu. That was many years ago. Many people had these at the time, but now they are mostly gone, lost or destroyed."

Perhaps because of not knowing Bronwen well, the man seemed reluctant to share much information about the medallion with her.

"But you have kept yours. Is it valuable? Whose face is pictured on it?"

"Perhaps we'll save that story for another time," Zayin replied guardedly. "I'm tired, and I need to rest. So should you."

Sitting beside him in the dim dungeon, Bronwen Llewellen suddenly knew for certain that there was something most unusual about the falcon medallion. She knew that the family of Richard Irons was involved with it, and she wondered how Irons could have been the "great visitor." But why would anyone honor a space pirate?

Captain Mark Edge and the Space Rangers arrived at the fortress's audience hall at the appointed time. It was a large room with a vaulted ceiling that seemed impossibly high. The walls were covered with paintings of the royal family going back far in time.

Edge greeted the young prince and introduced his companions. Dai and Ringo managed to perform courteously. The girls made elaborate curtsies, and all three noticeably kept their eyes fixed on the handsome prince as the captain went on.

"We are grateful that you chose to grant us this time, Prince Willuin," he said. "And I trust that we can be of service to you."

"You are welcome here, Captain Edge. You and all of your companions." Willuin then introduced his three large bodyguards.

Edge could hear Ringo whisper to Jerusha, "They

look like the Three Musketeers—carrying those swords and all."

The captain cast an annoyed glance at Ringo, then said, "Commandant Lee of Intergalactic Command has been concerned for your safety, Prince Willuin. She is afraid that you could be in some danger from . . . from the regent. We would like to put ourselves at your disposal if that would be possible."

The prince frowned. "Commandant Lee may be right about danger, of course. I have been kept here in the fortress for safety's sake, but I will have no real power—no authority to command—until the coronation."

"How do you know, then, what is taking place in the kingdom?" Edge inquired. "Through the regent?"

"The guide Gina Boyd has been my main source of information about the outside world. The regent comes here but seldom. In fact, very few people dare to venture into the Sylvan Timberlands at all. There are just too many dangers. Even here at the fortress, the guards have to be on alert twenty-four hours a day."

The big bodyguard Vav spoke up and said, "Indeed, sir, we have tried to persuade the prince not to travel publicly on this trip to the coronation, but he will not agree." He then said, "I would be happy to be your guide while you are here at the fortress."

The prince said, "That would be a fine arrangement. Visitors really need someone to protect them as well as guide them while they are at the fortress."

Raina said quickly, "We have Dai Bando here as our special protector. No one could be a better protector than Dai."

The young prince looked at Dai, and some understanding passed between the two. "I think you have made a good choice," he said. He turned back to the captain, saying, "Nevertheless, let my bodyguard Vav accompany you during your stay here."

At that point the prince looked directly at Mei-Lani, standing with the others and wearing the blue crystal attached to her belt. "And would you mind, Captain Edge, if the young lady Mei-Lani spent some time with me? I would appreciate it if she would explain to me some things about Intergalactic Command."

Edge asked, "Mei-Lani, is that fine with you?"

Mei-Lani looked embarrassed, but she nodded. "Of course, Captain, if it would be acceptable to you." And she agreed to accompany the prince for the few days before the caravan left for the palace.

Vav escorted Captain Edge and the Rangers to their quarters. Then he said, "You will have time to prepare yourself before dinner. It will not be for two more hours. I will be in the area. If you need help with anything, just call me."

It was likely that Jerusha made up her mind at once to need help with something.

Dai had made friends with the big guard and now decided to stroll around with Vav.

But Ringo had been thinking about his experience with the serpent in the forest. He had been thinking mostly about when he woke up and had happily managed to kiss Raina. *Maybe*, he thought, *I can figure out a way to stop breathing again.*

Prince Willuin and Mei-Lani wandered through the fortress. He did not ask her the questions about Intergalactic Command that she had expected him to ask, though. Instead, he showed her a great many things of interest in the stronghold and then began asking about her personal history. "Where do your people come from?" he inquired.

"Well, they both died when I was very young."

"Oh. I'm sorry to hear that."

"I hardly remember them. They were archeologists who worked for Intergalactic Command."

"Where did they do their work?"

"One place was the Draco constellation They visited there a long time ago, trying to find out about the existence—or nonexistence—of the White Dragon."

The prince seemed very interested in this, and he asked many other questions. After hearing what she had to say, he said, "Perhaps we could visit the Royal Library tomorrow. It may be possible that your parents' visit is recorded there. Would that interest you?"

Mei-Lani's eyes flew open. "Oh, that would be wonderful! I've so hoped to find out something about them."

"Then we will certainly do that." The prince then asked, "And where, may I ask, did you get that crystal?" And he indicated the blue object she wore on her belt.

Mei-Lani glanced down at the crystal. "I first saw it on a shelf in Gina Boyd's shop. She gave it to me."

"May I look at it?"

"Of course." She removed the crystal from its mounting and handed it to him.

Prince Willuin traced the carved letters with a finger and then looked up at her. "Do you understand these symbols?"

"Not yet, but I'm working on it. Actually, languages are my specialty. I hope to someday interpret what this crystal says."

"No one on SharNu has ever been able to decipher these. It would indeed be helpful to us if you could do so."

"Have you ever looked through one of these crystals?" she asked him.

At once Prince Willuin appeared nervous. He shook his head and said quickly, "You must never do that, Mei-Lani."

"Oh? Why not? I've already done so. It was an interesting sight."

"Please promise me you will not do it again." The prince was very agitated now. He added, "These crystals, I think, could be an interdimensional link of some kind. They are said to reveal truth. A few scientists who have studied them have gone mad. Whatever one sees through the crystals should perhaps not be seen by human beings in this dimension."

"Then I'll be very careful, Prince Willuin."

"I truly think it would be better for my people if they were banned. But there are too many of them on the planet for that to happen, and the people have a strong attraction to them."

Mei-Lani said, "Maybe they find that looking through them has an enhancing effect on one's mind."

"What do you mean?"

"When I looked through this crystal, I could feel *something* very strongly. It made me feel powerful, somehow, and larger. It's hard to explain . . ." She hesitated, then said, "I haven't mentioned this to Captain Edge . . . or to anyone else."

"What you say makes me all the more certain that you shouldn't experiment anymore. You will want your crystal back, but please be careful."

"Yes, I do want to study the hieroglyphics—but I promise not to look through it again."

"I think that would be very wise, Mei-Lani." He smiled warmly and gave her the crystal. "I would be heartbroken if anything happened to a young lady like you."

10

Masa's Orders

When Mei-Lani returned to her quarters, she was bombarded with questions from Raina and Jerusha. "What was he really like?" Jerusha wanted to know.

"He's . . . he's very nice."

"Is that all you can say?" Raina frowned. "What did you talk about? What did he say? What did you say?"

Mei-Lani did not want to reveal what had gone on with the crystal so she said, "He told me that tomorrow he was going to take me to the Royal Library. There might be some record there of my parents' visit."

"But did he say anything else?" Raina asked. "Is he interested in you?"

Mei-Lani suddenly felt defensive. "Sometimes I think you two forget that we're Space Rangers. We're not out here to play a part in some romantic story. Why don't you forget about all that romance stuff?"

"You just wait until you get a little older," Raina said knowingly. "You'll be exactly the same way."

At that moment a knock came on the door.

Mei-Lani opened it to reveal Vav standing there. "If you ladies are ready, I will escort you to the banquet."

"We're ready," Jerusha said quickly. "Come on, girls."

In the corridor they were joined by Captain Edge, Dai, and Ringo. They followed their escort until they arrived at a very large hall.

"This looks like the hall I once saw in an old *Robin Hood* movie back in Oldworld," Jerusha said wonderingly.

"I saw that movie. It does look like that hall," Ringo said with astonishment.

The room was carved out of stone and rose high above them. The floor was covered with carpet, thick and deep, and the smell of delicious food was in the air. Long tables had been placed in front of a main table set on a platform. Vav directed them to that special table.

"Oh, see, there are place cards!" Mei-Lani said. "Let's find where we're going to sit."

The Rangers found their places easily enough, but when Raina saw that Mei-Lani's seat was right next to the prince's chair, she sniffed. "It would be better if I sat there!"

"Or me!" Jerusha said.

But the girls were both farther down the table. Captain Edge was seated one seat down from the prince's place, while Ringo and Dai would sit directly across from him.

Many servants began carrying in the food. Apparently it was going to be a sumptuous meal. The *Daystar* crew all watched hungrily as the silver trays and goblets were placed on the table.

"I'm so hungry I could eat a dragon," Ringo announced.

Mei-Lani stood politely with everyone else when the prince entered and came to his place. "Be seated, my friends," he said. But he himself remained standing.

Then Mei-Lani—and surely all the Space Rangers and Captain Edge as well—was startled when the prince said in a loud, clear voice, "Our God, we thank You for this food. We thank You for every blessing You have given us. We know that every good gift comes from You. In the name of the Lord Jesus Christ we give You thanks."

Mei-Lani turned to the prince as soon as he sat

down. "Why didn't you tell me you were a Christian? Dai and Raina and Jerusha and I are, too!"

The prince shrugged. "Most of the people here know that I am a believer, but I am cautious about talking too much about Jesus publicly."

"Why is that?"

"Because if I did, there are some who would merely pretend to be His followers to gain my favor. My father wanted all of his subjects to have complete freedom in their choice of belief, and I have tried to follow his example."

"I think that's wonderful, prince." Mei-Lani smiled. "Has it worked out well?"

"I'm sorry to say that one of the things Lansur did upon becoming regent was to do away with public prayer to Jesus Christ in government buildings and schools."

"That's a terrible thing!"

"He called it the separation of church and state. But the problem is that the only religion that is excluded is the Christian faith. My research has shown that at one time it was like that in Oldworld. Is that not true? Only the Christian faith was forbidden? It was a direct attack on the truth of Jesus Christ, and a great wrong was done."

"It certainly was. I studied that in history. The people who wanted to forbid prayer had no problem if it was a prayer to Buddha. Only prayer to Jesus."

"Well, I believe everyone should have the right to believe as he wishes, but the regent has persecuted many who would not be quiet about their faith."

"When you are king," Mei-Lani said, "things will be different."

The prince looked at her. "Yes. If I can survive long enough to wear the crown, things will be different."

* * *

"No matter how many times I look at it, I never get used to it," Masa said.

"It scares the wits out of anyone who sees it," his hired helper Jobok replied.

Jobok and his fellow troopers were hired soldiers from Rastaban. They cared only for money. Jobok himself was a swarthy fellow with a deep scar over his right eye. Part of his left ear was missing, along with three fingers on his right hand. He wore frayed clothes and looked like a buccaneer. He was not pleasant to look at.

Masa had hired these rough men to fly a spaceship that had been manufactured to somewhat resemble a white dragon. Even its leathery looking wings flapped when the ship was flying. The nose looked like the head of a fierce lizard, and a long sinewy tail twisted back and forth behind the ship. The total effect appeared quite real.

Masa continued in his pushy way. "Attack the prince's caravan tonight. Make sure that you destroy it along with everyone in it." He touched the wing of the spacecraft. "Especially the prince. If you don't kill him, the whole deal is off."

"Don't you worry about us. You just have our money ready."

Masa felt a twinge of fear, but he said, "No need to make threats. I'll have the money waiting for you. Just be sure that your attack makes the people think they are being attacked by the White Dragon."

"We've never let you down yet, have we? I've got this dragon thing down to a fine art."

As Masa turned to leave, he said tersely, "Lansur has powerful friends on Rastaban. Again, do not fail—

or you will find yourself in fear of losing something worth far more than money."

Jobok nodded in agreement, then began shouting orders. "Men, get the ship ready. There's dark work to be done tonight."

11

The Graves on Ice Mountain

The caravan that would escort Prince Willuin to his coronation was assembling itself between two of the three great pyramids that supported the fortress Draconia. Hundreds of fortress dwellers in gala outfits ran to and fro like an army of giant ants.

The prince himself had organized and would lead the trip to his father's ancient palace in Ingara. While he was yet a small boy, the king had taught him that a good leader must first be a true servant of the people.

Soon the trumpets blew, and the Path Finders emerged from beneath the fortress. It would be their job to clear a trail through the dense jungle of the Sylvan Timberlands to the Royal Palace of the Ancients, many miles away. The task was not easy and would easily deplete men of lesser strength. But these were surely the largest men on the planet. And to the last man, the Path Finders apparently liked their job. As a result of their efforts, their beloved prince would soon be king.

Finally the prince completed establishing the proper order of the caravan. He placed soldiers around the perimeter, with reserves at the ready in case the procession was attacked. Many wagons were decorated in festive colors, mostly in light blue and dark orange combinations. They were heavily laden with all kinds of exotic foods for the celebration. A host of people held giant banners skyward.

Then Prince Willuin nodded at Vav. "It's time," he said.

95

"Forward, Path Finders," Vav shouted above the noise of the crowd. "Take us to Ingara."

The Path Finders raised their long swords and began slashing a wide trail through the thick forest. Once they started picking up speed, they were like a human machine that crunched up the vegetation, making it into a carpeted path.

Vav, Yod, and Kaph sooner or later made themselves visible to everyone in the caravan. Their presence added the sense of security that the people would need as they traveled farther into the jungle.

Captain Edge read scans from his datacorder. "Dai, everything appears OK for now, but I have a special assignment for you."

"What, Captain?"

"Stay close to the prince. I know his three bodyguards would not let anything happen to him—unless they were dead." Edge looked deep into Dai's eyes. "No matter what happens, if Prince Willuin's life is in danger, grab him and race back to Draconia."

"Aye, sir." Dai said. He blended into the crowd and made his way to the prince's location.

Bronwen had grown weary of the cell. The darkness, the smell, and the sense of the walls closing in on her made it almost unbearable. Periodically, guards opened the door, and the prisoners were briefly let out. But she had little idea of how much time had passed, for no sun was visible. It seemed she had been imprisoned weeks, yet she knew it could not have been that long.

She had grown close to her fellow prisoner, Zayin, and he seemed glad for her company as well. He must have been lonely in the cell all alone. He had had many interesting experiences in his full life that he related to her.

Once Bronwen asked him, "What more do you know about the White Dragon, Zayin?"

He raised his head and ran his fingers through his beard. "There used to be thousands of large reptiles on SharNu back in the ancient days. But no more."

"But what happened to them?"

"They were hunted to extinction by invaders from another planet."

"Which planet was that?"

"A planet called Rastaban."

"Ah, yes, I know Rastaban. A rather unpleasant race, those Rastabanians. But why did they hunt the dragons? Surely not to eat."

"Oh no. They believed that a powder made from the remains of the dragons brought about miraculous healing effects. They also believed there was the magic of eternal youth in the bones of white dragons—that if one ate a mixture of their bones with other elements, he would become forever young."

"That's always been the hope of man, Zayin. There was a man in Oldworld—Ponce de Leon—who went looking for the Fountain of Youth."

Zayin laughed softly. "I would wager he never found it."

"No, he never found it. God has given man a certain number of days, and that is all he will ever have."

"I wish that all men had the wisdom to see that. I wish people did not yearn so for what God did not intend for them to have," he said sadly.

"It always seemed sad to me," Bronwen said, "to watch men and women trying to preserve their youth. There is a dignity in growing old gracefully, and it always seemed tragic to me to see an older woman wearing the clothes of one very young. Or of an older man trying to go back and behave like a teenager again.

God wishes us to simply live our lives, and aging is a part of it."

"It saddens me about the white dragons. I have been told they were actually rather gentle creatures that simply had the ability to fly."

"Back on my home planet in Oldworld there were once huge herds of buffalo—great animals—millions of them. But most of those also were slain."

The two sat silently then until Zayin suddenly said, "I once heard that there is still one white dragon in the mountains."

"Do you really think that is so?"

"There have been reports from highly reliable people. But if there is one white dragon still existing, he is very crafty, because he has avoided capture. It is said that people see him only at night." He sighed. "I would like to see a white dragon before I die."

"Perhaps you will, Zayin," Bronwen said softly. "Perhaps you will. And perhaps God is planning something even better for you."

On another wide shelf down in the cave canyon of Ice Mountain, the party led by Tara Jaleel and Studs Cagney stared in silence at a row of mounds in the earth. The scene was creepy, for all the mounds had small crude boulders for headstones. Above several markers were swords, planted point first into the frozen ground. Some also bore helmets.

The grunts were extremely nervous, and Myron muttered, "I'd just as soon not stay around here."

Jaleel studied the mysterious mounds thoughtfully. "These have to be graves," she said. "But who were the people, and who buried them? And why here?"

Studs bent over one of the mounds. "This one was a leader," he said. "Look at the helmet and the sword.

Maybe the king himself? Probably the gas overcame them before they could go any farther. But you're right, Tara. Who were they, and who buried them? Some survivors probably. But then what happened to the survivors?"

Studs walked to the edge of the cliff-side trail then and looked downward. "I don't think anything could exist farther down in this hole," he reported. "The gas is so dense that it looks almost solid down there."

"Perhaps we'll find some answers later on," Studs said. "We'd better get back to the *Daystar*."

As the group prepared to climb back to the surface, Jaleel grumbled, "How are we going to get Heck back up? He's so heavy that he'll never make this climb."

"Don't worry about me!" Heck cried defiantly. "I'll beat you all back to the top."

"I doubt that, Heck," Studs said. "I doubt if you can make it fifty feet, much less a thousand. But if worse comes to worst, the grunts will get you back to the ship."

"I don't need anybody's help!" Heck growled. "I can take care of myself."

"Well, don't worry if you can't make it," Myron told him, anyway. "That's what grunts do. We learn in grunt school how to move great weights."

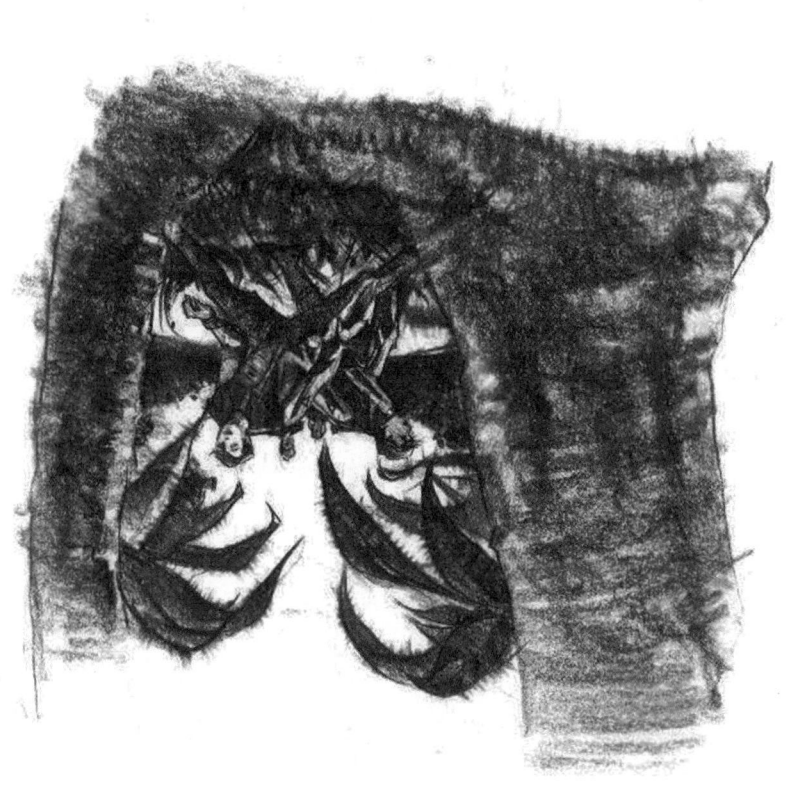

12

The Night People

Captain Edge thought he had not been around this many people in a long time. The crowd's happiness was contagious. He found himself whistling—and laughing at the simplest things.

Entertainment was provided as the caravan moved along. Right now he was watching a man try to juggle six white doves at the same time. What was astounding was the way the birds usually stayed still while being thrown into the air. But once in a while the juggler would just about have the whole performance coordinated when one bird would fly off, completely spoiling his timing. The rest of the doves would then drop to the ground like rocks, and the juggler would scurry around trying to gather them up.

The captain was watching a group of brightly clothed dancers when his nose picked up a strange odor. Jerusha stood nearby, and she must have smelled the foul odor at the same time. They exchanged glances. Then the captain strained his eyes to see into the forest.

"What we smell is trouble, Jerusha. I don't know what it is yet, but that smell is getting stronger."

"How come nobody else seems to notice it?" she asked.

Edge looked toward the prince, who was now standing and gazing toward the front of the caravan. "Willuin notices it."

At that moment the sound of a trumpet filled the air.

"Jerusha," Edge ordered, "gather the other Space Rangers quickly and form around the prince. It's my guess that we've just entered harm's way."

The blaring trumpet filled the air with a message that only Vav and Prince Willuin understood.

"I was hoping we would have made more progress before this happened," Willuin murmured to his bodyguard. "Check it out, and report back to me. If the enemy is nearby, we must be on the alert."

"Yes, sire." Vav ran ahead to the Path Finders. The sinews on his body resembled an orchestra in motion as he sped away. He took only moments to reach the trail breakers and find Tobias, their leader, bending close to the ground. Other Path Finders were also busily examining the forest floor—looking, they said, for telltale signs of someone they had hoped they wouldn't meet—the Night People.

As Vav approached, Tobias placed his index finger straight up over his closed lips. Then, using hand signals, he gathered the other Path Finders around him. Each man continued to keep an eye on the forest. Tobias and the Path Finders talked quietly together in a language that had come into being ages before. It was the language of the Ancients. Only these special men were permitted to use that sacred language. Vav didn't understand a word they said.

Then Tobias took Vav by the arm and drew him away from the others.

"The Night People are near," Tobias said. "Very near. And there is a large number of them."

"Are we in immediate danger?" Vav asked. "Or do we have time to move on?"

"There is no time. I'm surprised they haven't already begun their attack." Tobias peered at the jungle floor again. "Normally, it is very difficult to spot their tracks, but not tonight. See? There must be so many that they are not afraid of our knowing they are here."

Vav looked hard into the forest. "I can't see a thing."

"Use your sense of smell," Tobias advised.

"I know. I can smell them. That bad odor. It smells like rotting animals."

"Because, of course, it *is* the smell of rotting animals. The Night People place the decaying corpses of animals on their bodies. They think this gives them the power of the forest and makes them unbeatable." Tobias drew Vav close to him. "Alert the prince at once!"

Vav well knew that the Night People always protected their territory fiercely. They believed that glory in their future life could be realized only by the defeat of their enemies' warriors.

Even as Vav raced back to the prince, he heard the Night People begin their war chant. They sounded like a thousand screaming banshees. Now he could see the ordinary citizens fleeing to the rear.

Soon the only ones who remained at the front of the caravan were Prince Willuin's soldiers. Each man stood in place, waiting for the attack. The drums of the Night People began to thunder in rhythmical beats. The beating grew faster and faster. The soldiers could only brace themselves for the attack everyone knew was coming.

Then the enemy swarmed into the clearing, and the fight was on. The savage invaders used clubs and spears. They were people of the forest and carried no technological weapons.

The prince absolutely refused to flee with Dai. So Captain Edge and the Space Rangers encircled him, firing their Neuromags as fast as their fingers could pull the triggers.

High in the sky, a dragon shape circled in a wide sweep. Its wings moved in a flapping motion, and flame shot from its mouth. Masa's hired troops readied themselves for their attack.

"This is easier than I thought," Jobok said to his pilot as the two looked down on the forest below. The Path Finders had beaten a trail through the thick vegetation, letting the caravan's exact location be found in an instant. "The sun has almost set. Keep circling until night falls. We don't want them to see us—yet."

The pilot turned his attention to the viewer. "Look at this, sir!" he said excitedly.

"The Night People have attacked the caravan!" Jobok cried. "How lucky can we be? We'll wait until they finish their attack, then we'll go in and finish the business. That will satisfy Masa. He will have the Night People as well as the White Dragon to blame for Prince Willuin's death."

The two swarthy men smiled in satisfaction at their good fortune.

13

The Dragon Ship

Tara Jaleel checked her datacorder readout. "We need to get moving and right now. The force of the gas has made this shelf unstable. If it collapses now, we're all dead."

In fact, the gas was now rushing by so fast that it looked like a solid column.

"No one could have possibly gone deeper into this chasm. Let's move out, Studs," Jaleel said.

"Start back up," Studs Cagney ordered his grunts, glancing up at the close-to-vertical climb. "Heck, you lead the way."

"I'm not leading anything!" Heck said. "You guys go ahead. I'll bring up the rear."

The communication links in the envirosuits erupted in a frenzy of noise. All the grunts seemed overcome with uncontrollable laughter.

"Heck," Myron said patiently, "if we let you do that, you'll stay down here with the king over there." Myron looked over at the leader's grave. "No disrespect meant, sir."

"Heck, just get started!" Studs thundered. "Obey orders for once. It's going to take all of us to get you back to the top of this canyon."

Heck led the way up for about twenty-five feet before he was out of breath and filling the visor of his envirosuit with steam. Myron and the rest of the grunts tried the best they could to help him, but the ascent was steep and the path slippery. For every step they took forward, they seemed to fall two steps back. After a while, the whole group was back on the shelf.

"I guess they didn't teach you guys enough in grunt school, did they?" Heck Jordan jeered.

Jaleel, who had worked as hard as anyone to get Heck Jordan up the side of the canyon, stood in his face, visor to visor. "Go ahead and laugh. Look where you are. If we can't get you out of here, you're a dead man."

Heck kept on laughing. "Like I said to begin with, I'll take the rear position. Don't worry about me."

But Jaleel had had enough. "Studs, take the grunts back to the ship. Have Zeno contact Captain Edge and tell him our dilemma. Maybe *he* knows a way we can get this whale out of here."

At Studs Cagney's order, the grunts began working their way back up the treacherous path.

While Studs watched their progress from the shelf, Heck Jordan quietly removed the antigrav unit from his pouch, put on the device, and walked up behind Studs. Suddenly he gave the crew chief a bear hug, flipping the unit's controls at the same time. In an instant, the two of them were rocketing toward the top of the canyon.

The whole event took scarcely more than a few seconds. It was a lot quicker, in fact, than Heck had expected.

He lowered himself and Studs Cagney near *Daystar*. Studs collapsed on the ground as Zeno Thrax rushed from the ship to offer help. "I'm going down after the rest of them, First," Heck reported as he adjusted the antigrav unit to fly back down into the canyon

One by one, Heck brought up the whole team. No

one was laughing at him now. Heck's brain had saved them all a lot of very hard work.

After Heck had set down Tara Jaleel, however, she almost cracked his visor with the blow she inflicted on him.

"Don't you ever do that again, Ensign!" Jaleel was just barely able to control her rage. "I don't intend to be manhandled by anyone."

"What's the matter?" Studs asked. He had been watching the rescue of his crew. "What happened?"

"I told him that I didn't need his help and that I was more than able to climb that cliff all by myself," Jaleel snapped.

"And you turned your back on him, didn't you?" Studs grinned.

"Then he grabbed me, and in the next instant I'm hundreds of feet in the air." She glared at Heck, her eyes burning like flames. "I'm going to thrash you like the yard dog you are, anyway."

Heck looked at Zeno Thrax. The first officer still appeared to be amazed at what he had seen. Perhaps he was thinking that Heck's antigrav device alone could make Heck Jordan wealthy for the rest of his life. That's what Heck was thinking.

But Thrax only said, "We don't have time for any more of this, Tara. Something is happening with the caravan. We have to leave as soon as possible."

The *Daystar* zipped over the treetops and headed straight south toward the Sylvan Timberlands.

Zeno Thrax touched a communications button, saying, "Thrax to Captain Edge! Thrax to Captain Edge!"

There was a moment's silence, and then a garbled message came through. It was filled with static, and Thrax made an adjustment.

"Once again, Captain. I couldn't read you."

"This is Edge. What's going on, Thrax?"

"The *Daystar*'s scanners have picked up a large object flying toward your position. What's happening there, sir?"

"We're in the middle of a firefight here with some folks called the Night People."

"Shall I come?"

"No. We can handle it. I'm more concerned about that object you're talking about. What kind of an object?"

Zeno explained, and when Edge spoke again there was doubt in the captain's voice. "Do you suppose it could be that White Dragon?"

"Negative, sir. It's a craft made out of metal, and it's powered by engines."

"Well, that's a relief," Edge said. "I'll take a fight with a ship over a dragon anytime."

"Yes, sir. Me too, sir. What shall I do?"

"Intercept the dragon ship, First. Blow it out of the sky! It's a far greater danger to the caravan then the Night People. Over and out."

Thrax at once touched another button, and a loud clanging alarm went off. "Battle stations! All hands to battle stations! We will intercept the enemy shortly! All hands to battle stations!"

"I should have expected something like this," Tara Jaleel muttered. "White Dragon—my foot! It's just a ship designed to *look* like a dragon." The weapons officer glanced over her console. "Just give me a second here. I need to adjust the turbo cannons to full force."

"Hold up a minute, Lieutenant!" Thrax used rank with Tara to let her know he meant what he said. "They haven't actually done anything yet—except fly the thing."

He tried again to communicate with the strange

craft. "Zeno Thrax to white dragon ship . . ." But he received no reply after several attempts, so he said, "Be advised that this is the Intergalactic Command cruiser *Daystar.* If you do not heed our hail, then we will be forced to open fire with our turbo cannons."

In seconds, Zeno was looking at a face on the forward viewer. The man introduced himself as Jobok, then said, "Why are you interfering with our flight plan? We are only trying to honor Prince Willuin at his coronation. This ship was designed in his honor." The man could not have looked more insincere.

"I will say this only once," Zeno told him. "Your ship has no registry. The caravan is under attack, and we can only assume that your plans are hostile. Under the circumstances, I will give you fifteen seconds to vacate this air space. Thrax out."

On board the dragon ship, the pilot fumed. "That was the ugliest humanoid I have ever seen," he muttered to Jobok.

"Listen, you thick head. Ugly or not, that pilot just saved our lives by his warning. This ship is nothing compared to his. Now get us out of here."

Back on the *Daystar*'s bridge, the crew cheered as the white dragon ship rocketed off into space.

"What's their heading?" Zeno asked.

"Rastaban, sir," Jaleel growled. Her voice hissed like a snake's.

She was always cross when she missed a chance to do battle.

"Good. No need to kill unless we have to." Thrax maintained his bearing as first officer. "Ivan, take the helm and take us to the caravan. I'm going to contact Captain Edge."

14

Trapped

Jobok to Masa."

Masa answered the hail. "Go ahead. Has the caravan been destroyed?"

Lansur waited eagerly at Masa's side. He fully expected a positive response.

"That is a very *big* negative. Why didn't you tell me there was an Intergalactic Command cruiser patrolling around here? We almost were blown out of the sky."

Lansur couldn't believe his ears.

"We had no idea an Intergalactic cruiser was in the area!" Masa told Jobok.

"Well, the whole deal is off. Forget it. We're headed back to Rastaban. My advice to you is to get away while you can. I don't know who the captain of that cruiser is, but I wouldn't want to be the one to cross him. Jobok, out."

In seconds Masa was running as fast as his stumpy little legs could take him. He resembled a weasel fleeing from a chicken coop. His long robe trailed in the breeze behind him.

Regent Lansur watched him go, then took one last look at the throne in the Royal Hall of the Ancients. He realized that the object of his desire—being the ruler of SharNu—was now gone. He knew that if he stayed, he was a doomed man.

"Wait!" he called after Masa. "Wait for me!"

"Every man for himself." Masa's reply echoed behind him.

The two men arrived at their escape ship, breathless. It was not a large craft but large enough. It would carry them to Rastaban.

Lansur took his seat in the captain's chair. Masa sat nearby and glowered at him.

"Some ruler you turned out to be. I can't believe I went in with you," Masa complained.

"Listen, weasel. Anything you did, you did for yourself. You're no better than I. Now sit over there and fly this thing. I need time to adjust the Star Drive controls."

Masa took the helm and guided the craft toward the Cloud of Unknowing.

The men of Prince Willuin's caravan fought valiantly. The soldiers and the Path Finders bravely battled their attackers with their swords and spears. It was the Space Rangers with their sophisticated weapons, though, who tipped the scale against the Night People. The Rangers rendered several hundred of the Night People helpless with their Neuromags, which were set on stun. The Neuromag was a weapon the prince found very interesting.

"Vav, it looks like the remainder of the Night People are gathering over there," Willuin said to his bodyguard, pointing across the clearing. "Take reinforcements and gather them up."

Then the prince turned to Captain Edge and the Space Rangers. "Thank you. Without your help, my coronation would have turned into my funeral." His eyes brimmed with tears as he shook each one's hand.

"Prince Willuin," Edge said, "we've just received a most interesting message."

"Yes, Captain Edge?"

"My first officer has reported that the 'white dragon' your people have been seeing is not a dragon at all. Rather, it is actually a cleverly designed ship that mimicked the look of a white dragon."

"Well, it certainly served its purpose. All my people are terribly afraid on account of it."

"Thrax to Edge."

"Edge here."

"Captain, we're on our way. We estimate arrival in ten minutes. We need your coordinates so we don't fire on you."

"New orders, First. Hold a minute."

Edge looked at the prince. "Sire, with your permission, I would like to send the *Daystar* to the palace to check on Bronwen Llewellen and to arrest your regent."

"Of course." The prince nodded his head in agreement.

"Thrax, did you copy that?"

"Aye, sir. We're on our way. I hope there's a fight."

"Why is that?" Edge asked in disbelief. He knew his first officer liked to avoid trouble if he could.

"Jaleel."

"Understood. Edge out." The captain could easily imagine the frustration that was on his weapons officer's face.

Prince Willuin turned to Tobias then. "Everything is under control now? I thank you for your diligence."

"I'm here to serve, Your Majesty." Tobias's voice cracked with emotion. Obviously he truly loved his young prince. Then he stood tall and shouted, "Start the Path Finders! Let everyone rejoice! Let the minstrels play! By tonight we will have a king!"

And once again, the royal caravan pushed forward into the forest.

* * *

The *Daystar* set down in the great open area that stretched before the palace, and Zeno Thrax dispatched the grunts with all speed.

"Studs, report back to me as soon as you find Bronwen," he ordered. "Heck, you go with Studs and Jaleel and arrest Regent Lansur and Masa."

Tara Jaleel groaned.

Studs knew she never wanted to be stuck with Heck. Studs, on the other hand, did not mind. He always said that Heck Jordan could be ingenious and even helpful—at times.

After a period of searching, Myron reported back to Studs. They had found Bronwen, he said. The navigator was being held in a dungeon cell deep in the bowels of the palace. They had a problem, though, Myron said. They couldn't open the door. It had been fused shut.

"But I'll take care of it," Studs radioed Thrax.

In a few minutes Studs Cagney, along with a winded Heck Jordan arrived at the cell.

"Stand back," Studs told his men as he tried to see through the bars. The light in the cell was very dim. "Bronwen, is anyone in there with you?"

"Yes. One man. Zayin. A man who used to mentor the prince when he was much younger."

"Well, stand back from the door, both of you."

Studs adjusted the setting of his Neuromag. Then he aimed at the locking mechanism of the cell door and let loose a blast. The lock melted down to a pool of metal on the rock floor.

Studs pushed open the cell door. "Careful of that metal now. It's hot enough to give you a bad burn."

Bronwen Llewellen met him joyfully. Her companion, on the other hand, seemed reluctant to step out.

Bronwen went back into the cell and took his hand. "It's all right, Zayin. You can come out now. You are free."

"I know that," the man responded softly. "It's just that I have been in here for twelve long years. This place is not only my cell, but it has also become my home. Strange, is it not? I have dreamed about the day I would be free. I've practically gone insane thinking about freedom. And now, when the door to freedom is open, I find it hard to move my feet."

His response seemed to bring everyone almost to tears. Even Tara Jaleel.

While Lansur was trying to make sense of the Star Drive controls, Masa managed to fly their spacecraft into the Cloud of Unknowing.

"These Star Drive directions are useless," Lansur declared finally.

Masa looked at him with contempt. "That would be about the same thing I think about you."

Without looking up, Lansur replied angrily. "Masa, you've always been a weasel, and a weasel you will remain. And just what are we doing in the Cloud of Unknowing?"

Masa swung his fist, knocking the datacorder from Lansur's hands. "That felt good," he gloated. "I've wanted to do that for a long time."

Lansur grabbed a space wrench from the emergency kit and swung at his second in command.

Masa slumped to the deck, his eyes closed.

I've no more use for you, Lansur thought. He seized the limp Masa by his feet and dragged him to the ship's garbage disposal unit. Then he returned to the

115

bridge and took the pilot's seat. "Next time I empty the garbage, that will be the end of that rubbish Masa. Now, I need to get out of this cloud."

As the ship picked up speed and started its ascent, the viewer before him displayed not only the front of the ship but also either side. He stared at the viewer, horrified. His craft was leaving a wake in the dense cloud. That wake had attracted the attention of a glistening white dragon.

The dragon was enormous, easily larger than his small cruiser. It also turned out that the dragon could fly faster than the cruiser. In a moment, the creature had reached him. Lansur sat frozen in terror. The huge beast opened its mouth and closed its great teeth about the hull of his ship.

15

The Coronation

Bronwen, waiting with Zayin at the throne room doors, could see that the great hall was festooned with decorations. Gold and silver ornaments flashed, and red, green, and blue hangings covered the walls.

Suddenly a snarl of trumpets smote the air as ten men holding silver horns rose and blew mightily. From the other side of the hall, young Prince Willuin walked into the Royal Palace of the Ancients.

The prince was wearing his royal garments, and there was a serious look on his youthful face. He took his seat on the throne and gave a nod to his men.

The guards stepped aside then, and into the throne room stepped Bronwen with Zayin leaning on her arm. The man blinked at the splendor, but when the two stopped before the prince, a smile came to his lips and his eyes grew bright and warm.

Prince Willuin sat silent for a moment. He certainly had been told of their visit, but something about Zayin appeared to puzzle him. "You are welcome here, sir, and you too, madam."

"Thank you, my prince," Zayin said promptly, and he noticeably stood straighter.

Bronwen, watching, realized that her former cellmate was much taller than she had thought. In the dungeon, he had been so stooped that she had thought him to be a rather short man. Now he stood stiffly at her side, his head in the air. Also, she was accustomed to the beaten look on his face that she had known in the cell, but this was a different Zayin. A new Zayin. A free Zayin, perhaps.

Prince Willuin got to his feet. He approached his two visitors and, ignoring Bronwen Llewellen, stopped directly in front of the man. Silently, the two studied each other.

The prince found himself thinking, *What is it that is different about this man?* Aloud he said, "I can remember very little about you, Zayin. You were taken away when I was quite young, but I am most pleased to see you again."

"Thank you, Prince Willuin," Zayin replied. He stood looking at the prince, and something in his very look troubled Willuin. He felt uncomfortable but did not know why. "I would that my father were here to greet you," he said. "You were a great favorite of his, as I remember."

"Yes. That is true. I did feel I was favored by King Regur."

"Something is . . . different about you, Zayin, though I cannot say what it is. You seem not to be quite the Zayin I remember."

"Things change with time, my prince," the man said. He smiled and stood even more erect, unmoving.

Bronwen Llewellen must have seen the prince's puzzlement, for she asked, "Is something wrong, Prince Willuin?"

"No—*yes!*" Willuin kept his eyes focused on the man's face as he spoke. "Yes, there is. Something about this man puzzles me. My memories of my early teacher are vague, but somehow this one does not seem the same."

"Do you think he is an impostor, then?" she asked. "I found no harm in him."

"No, not an impostor. But at the same time, neither is he . . ."

Prince Willuin felt confused. He began to pace the floor as his visitors—and indeed everyone else—watched him closely. Finally he came back to them and said, "I've been very much against this use of the crystals, but for some reason I feel that I must break my own rule."

Reaching into the pouch at his side, Prince Willuin took out a blue crystal.

"Are you certain you want to do this?" the man asked gently.

The unexpected smile on his face, however, and something else about his countenance gave Prince Willuin confidence that he was about to do the right thing. "Yes, I am certain. I want to know the truth."

He lifted the crystal to his eyes then and through it gazed directly at the face of Zayin. He saw nothing for a moment, and then there was a swirling confusion of colors. He kept looking, and the features of the man appeared before him. Suddenly Willuin gave a loud cry.

Bronwen stepped to his side, and his bodyguards moved quickly forward. "What is it, my prince?" she asked anxiously.

Prince Willuin did not answer. He held the crystal in place before his eyes for a moment longer. He wanted to be sure of what he had seen—whom he had seen.

Lowering the crystal, Prince Willuin studied the man's face. Silence was all around and seemed thick enough to cut with a sword. Finally in a tight voice, Willuin asked, "Do you have the necklace?"

Zayin nodded. "Yes, I do." He had come dressed for the occasion in a suit of gray, and now he drew out the medallion from beneath his coat.

As soon as he did, Prince Willuin let out a glad cry.

He leaped forward and eagerly embraced the man. The two held each other tightly.

For a long moment they stood clasping each other, and then Willuin stepped back. Tears were in his eyes. "Do you not see?" he cried, addressing the confused throng in the throne room. "It is my *father!* It is the king! King Regur is back to rule over his kingdom!"

Instantly all of the king's subjects dropped to their knees, and a joyous shout went up. "King Regur! All hail the king!"

Bronwen Llewellen appeared to be totally bewildered. She stood looking from the prince to his father and back again. Finally she asked, "Is it truly you, King Regur?"

The man she had known as Zayin turned to face her. There was something kingly about him even now. "Yes, Navigator. When most of my party was lost in the North Polar Region, some of us survived. We buried our companions and then found our way back. But when Regent Lansur discovered that I was alive, he imprisoned me. From then on, I thought it safer to take Zayin's name. And now I am indeed back, but not to rule. I rejoice to see that I have a son worthy to replace me on the throne."

The prince shouted, "Quick! Send the word over the whole kingdom. *The king is back!*"

Almost at once, the bells began to ring, and people were celebrating in all the streets. "The king is back! King Regur is alive! Our king is with us again!"

The coronation of Prince Willuin took place in the palace's open courtyard. Every available space was filled. It appeared that all the attendees had worn their best clothes, and each made a splash of color in the morning sunshine. The ceremonies had already been in progress for two hours, but now the time had come for the crowning of the king.

Captain Edge, the *Daystar* Space Rangers, and the rest of the crew were all present. Even Contessa, Jerusha's dog, was there. The Rangers stood close enough to easily see what was going on.

Today King Regur wore garments of purple as he stood beside his son. The men of the council, all looking happy and content, were close by also.

Then King Regur stepped forward and gave a signal. Instantly trumpets sounded, sharp and loud and clear.

"My loyal subjects," King Regur began in a strong voice, "I welcome you here on this occasion. After my long absence I am happy to return and see that I left a child but now find a man strong and courageous and honorable."

The king looked fondly at his son, and the spectators cheered.

When the crowd quieted down, the king went on. "I am tired from my years of imprisonment, but my son, the prince, is young and strong. I believe it is time to give way to youth." He turned to Willuin and put a hand on his shoulder. "You are, indeed, a son worthy to be king, and I pronounce you this day King of SharNu."

Cheers sounded again.

It was a very solemn moment when the crown was placed on the prince's head and all the notables of the kingdom gave homage to their new ruler.

Captain Edge and his crew were watching with great pleasure when suddenly King Willuin called out, "Captain Edge, bring your people forward, please."

"Come on, gang," Edge said. "It seems we're about to officially meet the new monarch."

The crew of the *Daystar* gathered before the king,

and Willuin went down the line one by one, giving gifts and making a small speech of appreciation—just a word at times—to each of them.

The Rangers stood waiting their turn. Heck would be next, as soon as King Willuin finished talking with Studs Cagney.

The captain had told Heck Jordan and the other Rangers that they might dress as they pleased for this occasion, and Heck's outfit was a frightful clash of purple, green, red, blue, and pink. He was even wearing his antigrav unit. Perhaps the people of SharNu thought this was appropriate dress for others in the galaxy, but the *Daystar* crew had groaned when they saw him.

"You ought to be arrested for wearing an outfit like that," Ringo told him.

Heck didn't care. "You're just jealous," he answered.

Now suddenly the king was standing before him. "And this young man, I am told, is worthy of special honor. I would like—"

At that exact moment Heck felt Contessa brush up against him. That brief contact must have somehow flipped the switch of his antigrav unit to full power, for amazing things began to happen at once.

The king was about to place a hand on Heck's shoulder when Heck shot upward like a rocket. The king fell back. The bodyguards rushed toward him with a shout, probably assuming it was a plot against the new king.

Screams sounded from all over the crowd. Every neck craned backward to trace the flight of the purple, green, red, blue, and pink object that hurtled high over the castle.

Heck's twists and turns were so abrupt that he had

a hard time even finding the controls, much less adjusting them.

While Heck was still flying through the air, King Willuin approached Captain Edge. "What a remarkable demonstration of technology," he said with a wide smile. "I would like to see that again sometime."

The captain and everyone else gaped stupidly at him. Edge could hear Ringo muttering, "Bet he thinks Heck did that on purpose as a surprise for his coronation."

"He'll probably make Heck a knight," Raina's voice joined in.

Edge knew exactly what would happen. When Heck's antigrav unit brought him down to earth, Willuin would congratulate him with enthusiasm. The crew of the *Daystar* would never hear the last of this, and Heck would claim all the credit.

King Willuin was still smiling. He said to Captain Edge, "What a talented young man! I imagine you don't have many like him in your crew."

"No, Your Highness," Edge said with a straight face, "there isn't anyone like him."

"Well, we're looking forward to a long and lasting relationship with Intergalactic Command."

The grunts heard none of this. They were too busy laughing at Heck, who for the moment was floating around helplessly, seeming unable to return to earth.

"It couldn't have happened to a nicer guy," Myron said.

Even the Space Rangers had to laugh at that. They watched until Heck finally began to lose power and floated like a leaf back to the ground.

"Well, how did you like my demonstration?" Heck asked at once.

"Very wonderful indeed, Heck," the king said. "I am going to give you a special medal as a mark of my favor."

Heck winked at Raina. "You stick with me, kid," he said. "I'm going places."

16

The Discovery

The day after Willuin's coronation, several of the Space Rangers were relaxing in the royal gardens when Ringo Smith left the group and wandered off on his own. He rounded a corner, and there sat King Regur on a bench, admiring a rosebush.

"Ringo Smith?" King Regur addressed the boy. "Is that right?"

"Yes, sire."

"I understand that you have a medallion that you wear around your neck."

"Yes," Ringo answered sheepishly.

"May I see it?"

Ringo took off the medallion, and the former king inspected it closely. "Very interesting," he said. "Very interesting."

"Sire, I would give it to you," Ringo said, "but it wouldn't do any good."

"Why would you want to do that? This medallion is very old and probably has much value."

"Not to me, it doesn't."

"What?" the king replied, seeming startled. "This medallion is not important to you?"

Ringo was beginning to feel very uncomfortable. He was afraid the king wouldn't like him anymore if he knew that he was the son of Sir Richard Irons.

"My mother gave it to me before she died," he said. "I always loved it because it was hers and it's my only possession from her."

"Then, why . . ."

"I found out on one of my missions what the medallion really means."

"You did? Tell me what you found out." There was a hint of excitement in the king's voice.

At first Ringo hesitated, but then he decided to take a chance. "Have you ever heard of a space pirate by the name of Sir Richard Irons?"

"I'm afraid not. I haven't heard much of anything in twelve years. And before that, the queen was my whole life. In fact, we spent many hours together right in this spot."

"Well, I found out that the man on the medallion is Sir Richard Irons. And he's a space pirate—and he's my father!"

King Regur examined the image on Ringo's medallion. "So this man is your father?"

"Yes," Ringo acknowledged sorrowfully. "I fear so."

"If you're right, son, then he must be my father, too."

"But that's impossible! There's no—I don't mean to offend you, sire, but you are much older than this man."

"That is exactly my point."

"I don't understand." Ringo felt confused.

The kind king placed his hand on Ringo's shoulder and patted it reassuringly.

"I want to show you something." The king reached into his tunic and brought out an object. He held it out to Ringo. It was a medallion.

"But this is exactly like my medallion. Where did you get it?"

"I've had it since I was a small boy. My father gave it to me, but he told me the true story behind it."

"I know the true story. The face on the medallion is . . ." But Ringo suddenly was feeling totally confused.

Just then a messenger ran up to the king. "Sire, Prince Willuin requests your presence in the palace. He would like your judgment concerning the Night People. They are an unruly lot. He says you would know how to deal with them."

"Tell him I'll be right there."

When the messenger left, King Regur handed Ringo's medallion back to him and then placed his own inside his tunic.

"I must go now, Ringo," the king said. "I will tell you this much, though—the man pictured on our medallions is *not* Sir Richard Irons."

"If it's not my father, then who is it?" Ringo cried.

"He was a man who lived many years ago. He was a noble ancestor of yours, Ringo. He was Jeremiah Irons, the one who first brought the good news of Jesus Christ to our planet. Many of our people came to know and love Christ under his teaching. In honor of him, some engravers in my own family cast hundreds of these medallions. This tiny mark on the back is from our Craftsman's Guild. All my family members wear these. I didn't know any of them had ever left SharNu, though."

"I just don't understand," replied Ringo.

"I don't understand, either," King Regur answered, "but there must be an explanation for how the medallion came down to you. Your father obviously would have no interest in it. Your mother must have been a Christ-follower and wanted you to come to know Jesus. I believe that nothing happens by accident. God controls what happens. Perhaps together, we can somehow find out how your medallion came to her—and you."

"I would like that very much, Your Majesty."

King Regur smiled. "Perhaps the Lord Himself will reveal this mystery to you in due time."

The king strode away toward the palace then, and Ringo watched till he was out of sight.

Before heading toward *Daystar*, Ringo took out his medallion again and looked at the engraved face. He thought, *One good thing has already happened. I've learned there were Christian believers far back in my family.*

Dai Bando and the grunt Myron were taking a break from work in the cargo bay. Myron sat on a crate with his back against the bulkhead. He had been studying Dai, who sat across from him, whistling a little tune.

"I wish I could sing and whistle like you, Dai," the grunt said. "It must be nice."

"I never thought much about it. Guess I was singing when I was a baby."

Myron studied him a while longer, then said, "I've been thinking—there's only one mystery on SharNu that didn't get cleared up."

Dai raised his eyebrows. "What mystery is that?"

"Well, we found out about Lansur. He was a villain. The world is better off with him out of the way."

"I'll agree that he was a sad case. Evil always brings men down."

"And the prince is now the king. But what will the old king do? King Regur?"

"About what?"

"Well, he left to find his wife, Queen Daleth, and he didn't find her."

"No, he didn't."

"And we never found out what happened to her. You know what I think?" Myron asked. "I think he'll spend the rest of his life looking for her."

"He had a great love for his queen. That's for sure. But he'll see her again someday—even if he never finds her here."

"You mean in heaven, don't you?"

"Yes, that's one thing all Christians can look forward to. As a matter of fact, Christians really never have to say good-bye to each other."

After another pause, Myron asked, "What do you think of the king? I mean the new king."

"I think he is a fine example of what a follower of Jesus Christ should be."

Myron shifted uneasily. Then, suddenly, he said, "Tell me about this Jesus you keep talking about."

Dai Bando smiled. "I've been waiting for you to ask, Myron. Jesus is the Lamb of God. I'll explain what that means . . ."

Mei-Lani walked into the *Daystar*'s lounge area. She had decided to look out the portal for a few minutes.

Daystar had just left SharNu and was headed in the direction of Rastaban. The space outside the portal was black and star-filled. She fingered the blue crystal and knew that every time she did that she would think of SharNu and wonder about her parents. She had discovered nothing about them in the royal library.

Now as the *Daystar* rocketed smoothly through space, Mei-Lani thought, *I'm going to take one last look through this crystal and then never again. I'll look back at SharNu.*

Holding the blue object to her eyes, she saw that the universe seemed to be wavering. The stars in the blackness of the heavens quivered like dots of silver.

And then, without warning, something slammed into her line of vision. Mei-Lani gasped and blinked.

What she saw, back in SharNu's atmosphere, was a gigantic white dragon.

"It's a dragon," she whispered. "Really a white dragon." For a second she held the crystal in place. Startled, she took a step back, and she dropped the crystal. It shattered into a thousand pieces on the lounge deck. And out through *Daystar*'s rear portal, now she could see nothing but the planet Sharnu, rapidly growing smaller.

Mei-Lani looked at the scattered pieces of blue crystal. Then she said, "I'm glad that crystal broke. Some things it's better not to tamper with. That was one of them."

And suddenly wonder filled her heart. "So," she said softly, "I've found out something my parents never knew. The Draco constellation *does* have at least one white dragon, even if it doesn't get out into space."

After looking out for a long time, she swept up the pieces of broken crystal and deposited them into the waste tube. "That's over," she said. "Now I can put blue crystals out of my mind."

She found Heck and several grunts in the recreation area. Heck was dressed in his regular uniform but wore a medal around his neck. It was the medal given to him by King Willuin.

Heck was orating to the grunts, who were listening in awe. "And so the king and I have talked quite a bit about the future of SharNu, and we're going to get together on some things."

Mei-Lani joined them, smiling. "You'll never change, Heck."

"Change! Why should I change? I'm satisfied with me the way I am. Anybody wants to change, let them do it, but I'm staying the way I am. Exactly."

Mei-Lani sighed. "I guess you will, Heck. For the

time being." She sat down then and listened while Heck continued spinning his tale to the grunts.

Afterward, Myron had a big grin on his face as he walked past her. "Heck's story gets better every time he tells it."

Mei-Lani took a deep breath. "Some things will never change. But I'm still sure there's hope for Mr. Hector Jordan."

Get swept away in the many Gilbert Morris Adventures available from Moody Press:

"Too Smart" Jones

4025-8 Pool Party Thief
4026-6 Buried Jewels
4027-4 Disappearing Dogs
4028-2 Dangerous Woman
4029-0 Stranger in the Cave
4030-4 Cat's Secret
4031-2 Stolen Bicycle
4032-0 Wilderness Mystery

Come along for the adventures and mysteries Juliet "Too Smart" Jones always manages to find. She and her other homeschool friends solve these great adventures and learn biblical truths along the way. Ages 9-14

Seven Sleepers - The Lost Chronicles

3667-6 The Spell of the Crystal Chair
3668-4 The Savage Game of Lord Zarak
3669-2 The Strange Creatures of Dr. Korbo
3670-6 City of the Cyborgs

More exciting adventures from the Seven Sleepers. As these exciting young people attempt to faithfully follow Goél, they learn important moral and spiritual lessons. Come along with them as they encounter danger, intrigue, and mystery. Ages 10-14

Dixie Morris Animal Adventures

3363-4 Dixie and Jumbo
3364-2 Dixie and Stripes
3365-0 Dixie and Dolly
3366-9 Dixie and Sandy
3367-7 Dixie and Ivan
3368-5 Dixie and Bandit
3369-3 Dixie and Champ
3370-7 Dixie and Perry
3371-5 Dixie and Blizzard
3382-3 Dixie and Flash

Follow the exciting adventures of this animal lover as she learns more of God and His character through her many adventures underneath the Big Top. Ages 9-14

The Daystar Voyages

4102-X Secret of the Planet Makon
4106-8 Wizards of the Galaxy
4107-6 Escape From the Red Comet
4108-4 Dark Spell Over Morlandria
4109-2 Revenge of the Space Pirates
4110-6 Invasion of the Killer Locusts
4111-4 Dangers of the Rainbow Nebula
4112-2 The Frozen Space Pilot
4113-0 White Dragon of Sharnu
4114-9 Attack of the Denebian Starship

Join the crew of the Daystar as they traverse the wide expanse of space. Adventure and danger abound, but they learn time and again that God is truly the Master of the Universe. Ages 10-14

Seven Sleepers Series

3681-1   Flight of the Eagles
3682-X   The Gates of Neptune
3683-3   The Swords of Camelot
3684-6   The Caves That Time Forgot
3685-4   Winged Riders of the Desert
3686-2   Empress of the Underworld
3687-0   Voyage of the Dolphin
3691-9   Attack of the Amazons
3692-7   Escape with the Dream Maker
3693-5   The Final Kingdom

Go with Josh and his friends as they are sent by Goél, their spiritual leader, on dangerous and challenging voyages to conquer the forces of darkness in the new world. Ages 10-14

Bonnets and Bugles Series

0911-3   Drummer Boy at Bull Run
0912-1   Yankee Bells in Dixie
0913-X   The Secret of Richmond Manor
0914-8   The Soldier Boy's Discovery
0915-6   Blockade Runner
0916-4   The Gallant Boys of Gettysburg
0917-2   The Battle of Lookout Mountain
0918-0   Encounter at Cold Harbor
0919-9   Fire Over Atlanta
0920-2   Bring the Boys Home

Follow good friends Leah Carter and Jeff Majors as they experience danger, intrigue, compassion, and love in these civil war adventures. Ages 10-14

Moody Press, a ministry of the Moody Bible Institute,
is designed for education, evangelization, and edification.
If we may assist you in knowing more about Christ
and the Christian life, please write us without obligation:
Moody Press, c/o MLM, Chicago, Illinois 60610.